AF680656

Traffic Management Act 2004

CHAPTER 18

Explanatory Notes are available separately

GRAN*GIS* UK Publishing

Adapted and published by GRANGIS (Grand Register Library).
Online: www.grangis.com
E-mail: contact@grangis.com

© Crown Copyright
Contains public sector information licensed under the Open Government Licence v3.0.
You may re-use this publication free of charge in any format or medium. You must re-use it accurately and not in a misleading context.

© GRANGIS 2022.
In this version:
ISBN: 979-8-88559-054-9
Where we have identified any copyrighted material, you will need to obtain written permission for re-use.
Note: This is the original version (as it was originally enacted). Title, sub-title and the generated date is as marked on the page.

Traffic Management Act 2004

CHAPTER 18

CONTENTS

PART 1

TRAFFIC OFFICERS

Traffic officers for England and for Wales

Jurisdiction and powers of traffic officers

Miscellaneous and supplementary

PART 2

NETWORK MANAGEMENT BY LOCAL TRAFFIC AUTHORITIES

General duties relating to network management

Enforcement of network management duties

PART 3

PERMIT SCHEMES

PART 4

STREET WORKS

Enforcement

Co-ordination of works by street authority

Direction-making powers

Records and information

Miscellaneous

PART 5

HIGHWAYS AND ROADS

Strategic roads in London

Enforcement of certain offences under the Highways Act 1980

Records of objects placed in highway

Skips, scaffolding, building materials and excavations: charges for occupation of highway etc.

Traffic Management Act 2004

2004 CHAPTER 18

An Act to make provision for and in connection with the designation of traffic officers and their duties; to make provision in relation to the management of road networks; to make new provision for regulating the carrying out of works and other activities in the street; to amend Part 3 of the New Roads and Street Works Act 1991 and Parts 9 and 14 of the Highways Act 1980; to make new provision in relation to the civil enforcement of traffic contraventions; to amend section 55 of the Road Traffic Regulation Act 1984; and for connected purposes. [22nd July 2004]

BE IT ENACTED by the Queen's most Excellent Majesty, by and with the advice and consent of the Lords Spiritual and Temporal, and Commons, in this present Parliament assembled, and by the authority of the same, as follows:—

PART 1

TRAFFIC OFFICERS

Traffic officers for England and for Wales

1 Traffic officers: introduction

(1) This Part makes provision for the designation of individuals as traffic officers by, or under an authorisation given by, the Secretary of State or the Assembly.

(2) The duties assigned to traffic officers must be connected with, or intended to facilitate or to be conducive or incidental to—

(a) the management of traffic on the relevant road network; or

(b) the performance of any other functions of the appropriate national authority (in its capacity as a traffic authority or highway authority).

(3) In subsection (2) "the relevant road network" means—

(a) the network of relevant roads in England (in the case of traffic officers designated by, or under an authorisation given by, the Secretary of State); or
(b) the network of relevant roads in Wales (in the case of traffic officers designated by, or under an authorisation given by, the Assembly).

(4) Traffic officers shall have such special powers (for use in connection with the performance of their duties) as are referred to in section 5(1).

(5) In this Part "relevant road" means a road in England for which the Secretary of State is the traffic authority or a road in Wales for which the Assembly is the traffic authority.

2 Designation of traffic officers

(1) The appropriate national authority may—
(a) designate individuals as traffic officers; and
(b) authorise another person to designate individuals as traffic officers.

(2) An authorisation under subsection (1)—
(a) must be given (and may be varied or withdrawn) in writing; and
(b) may be given subject to such limitations and conditions as the appropriate national authority thinks appropriate.

(3) The designation of an individual as a traffic officer must be made (and may be withdrawn) in writing.

(4) A designation may provide that it is to remain in force (unless it is withdrawn or otherwise ceases to have effect) for a specified period.

(5) A traffic officer designated under an authorisation must be employed by, or by a person providing services to, the authorised person.

(6) An individual designated under an authorisation shall cease to be a traffic officer if the person who appointed him either withdraws his designation or ceases to be authorised.

(7) The appropriate national authority may direct an authorised person to withdraw immediately the designation of all or any of the individuals who have been designated by that person.

Jurisdiction and powers of traffic officers

3 Jurisdiction of traffic officers

(1) A traffic officer has jurisdiction—
(a) over any relevant road in England (if he was designated by, or under an authorisation given by, the Secretary of State); or
(b) over any relevant road in Wales (if he was designated by, or under an authorisation given by, the Assembly),

unless his designation provides that this subsection does not apply to him.

(2) If subsection (1) does not apply to a traffic officer, he has jurisdiction only over such relevant roads, or relevant roads of such descriptions, as may be specified in his designation.

4 Powers to direct traffic officers

(1) A traffic officer shall, when carrying out his duties, comply with any direction of a constable.

(2) Subject to that, a traffic officer designated by an authorised person shall, when carrying out his duties, comply with any direction of the appropriate national authority.

5 The special powers of a traffic officer

(1) For the purposes of this Part the special powers of a traffic officer are the following—
- (a) powers conferred by sections 6 and 7;
- (b) powers conferred by orders under section 8; and
- (c) powers conferred by or under any other Act which are expressed to be special powers for the purposes of this section.

(2) The exercise of those powers is subject to the following restrictions.

(3) Those powers may only be exercised for one or more of the following purposes—
- (a) maintaining or improving the movement of traffic on a relevant road over which the traffic officer has jurisdiction by virtue of section 3;
- (b) preventing or reducing the effect of anything causing (or which has the potential to cause) congestion or other disruption to the movement of traffic on such a road;
- (c) avoiding danger to persons or other traffic using such a road (or preventing risks of any such danger arising);
- (d) preventing damage to, or to anything on or near, such a road;

or for a purpose incidental to any of those purposes.

(4) Subject to that, those powers may be exercised—
- (a) on or in relation to any relevant road over which the traffic officer has jurisdiction to act by virtue of section 3; or
- (b) if the condition specified in subsection (5) is met, on or in relation to any other road in England and Wales.

(5) The condition is that the traffic officer is acting—
- (a) at the direction of the chief officer of police for the area in which the road is situated; or
- (b) with the consent of the traffic authority for the road.

(6) A traffic officer may not exercise his special powers on a road unless he is in uniform.

6 Powers to stop or direct traffic

(1) This section confers the following powers on a traffic officer—
- (a) a power, when the traffic officer is engaged in the regulation of traffic in a road, to direct a person driving or propelling a vehicle—
  - (i) to stop the vehicle, or
  - (ii) to make it proceed in, or keep to, a particular line of traffic;
- (b) a power, for the purposes of a traffic survey of any description which is being carried out on or in the vicinity of a road, to direct a person driving or propelling a vehicle—

(i) to stop the vehicle, or

(ii) to make it proceed in, or keep to, a particular line of traffic, or

(iii) to proceed to a particular point on or near the road on which the vehicle is being driven or propelled;

(subject to the restriction in section 35(3) of the Road Traffic Act 1988 (c. 52));

(c) a power, when the traffic officer is engaged in the regulation of vehicular traffic in a road, to direct persons on foot (or such persons and other traffic) to stop;

(d) a power to direct a person driving a mechanically propelled vehicle, or riding a cycle, on a road to stop the vehicle or cycle.

(2) In section 35 of the Road Traffic Act 1988 (drivers to comply with traffic directions)—

(a) in subsection (1)—

(i) after "a constable" there is inserted "or traffic officer";

(ii) after "duty" there is inserted "or the traffic officer (as the case may be)";

(b) in subsection (2)(b) after "constable" there is inserted "or traffic officer".

(3) In section 37 of that Act (directions to pedestrians)—

(a) after "uniform" there is inserted "or traffic officer";

(b) after "duty" there is inserted "or the traffic officer (as the case may be)".

(4) In section 163 of that Act (power of police to stop vehicles), in subsections (1) and (2) after "uniform" there is inserted "or a traffic officer".

(5) In Part 1 of Schedule 2 to the Road Traffic Offenders Act 1988 (c. 53) (prosecution and punishment of offences under the Traffic Acts), in column 5 of the entry relating to section 35 of the Road Traffic Act 1988 after "constable" there is inserted ", traffic officer".

7 Powers to place temporary traffic signs

(1) A traffic officer has the powers of a constable under section 67(1) of the Road Traffic Regulation Act 1984 (c. 27) (power in the case of emergencies and temporary obstructions etc. to place and temporarily maintain traffic signs on a road or on any structure on a road).

(2) The references in section 67(1) and (2) to powers conferred by subsection (1) of that section include a reference to the corresponding powers of a traffic officer by virtue of this section.

8 Power to confer further special powers on traffic officers

(1) The appropriate national authority may by order made by statutory instrument confer further special powers on traffic officers.

(2) The national authority may not confer a further special power on traffic officers unless it is satisfied that the power is necessary for the purpose of facilitating the performance of any duties which may be assigned to traffic officers.

(3) The order may—

(a) provide for the enforcement of any special power conferred by the order (whether by the creation of a summary offence or otherwise);

(b) make supplemental, incidental, transitional or consequential provision (including provision amending any Act or subordinate legislation).

(4) An order under this section may not be made by the Secretary of State unless a draft of the order has been laid before and approved by a resolution of each House of Parliament.

9 Removal of certain vehicles by traffic officers

(1) The power to make regulations under section 99 of the Road Traffic Regulation Act 1984 (c. 27) includes, in relation to the removal of vehicles by traffic officers, power to make consequential provision.

(2) The provision which may be made by virtue of subsection (1) includes in particular provision—

(a) amending, or

(b) applying in relation to vehicles removed by traffic officers (with or without modifications),

any provision of sections 100 to 102 of that Act (disposal of vehicles removed under section 99).

Miscellaneous and supplementary

10 Offences

(1) A person who assaults a traffic officer in the execution of his duties is guilty of an offence and liable, on summary conviction, to imprisonment for a term not exceeding 51 weeks or to a fine not exceeding level 5 on the standard scale (or both).

(2) A person who resists or wilfully obstructs a traffic officer in the execution of his duties is guilty of an offence and liable, on summary conviction, to imprisonment for a term not exceeding 51 weeks or to a fine not exceeding level 3 on the standard scale (or both).

(3) A person who, with intent to deceive—

(a) impersonates a traffic officer,

(b) makes any statement or does any act calculated falsely to suggest that he is a traffic officer, or

(c) makes any statement or does any act calculated falsely to suggest that he has powers as a traffic officer that exceed the powers he actually has,

is guilty of an offence and liable, on summary conviction, to imprisonment for a term not exceeding 51 weeks or to a fine not exceeding level 5 on the standard scale (or both).

(4) A person to whom this subsection applies who fails to give his name and address to a traffic officer in uniform on being required to do so by that officer is guilty of an offence and liable on summary conviction to a fine not exceeding level 3 on the standard scale.

(5) Subsection (4) applies to a person whom the traffic officer reasonably believes to have been the driver of a vehicle at a time of a failure to comply with—

(a) a direction given in relation to that vehicle under a power conferred by section 6, or

(b) the indication given by a traffic sign placed under a power conferred by section 7.

(6) In the case of offences committed before the commencement of section 281(5) of the Criminal Justice Act 2003—

(a) subsections (1) and (3) apply as if for "51 weeks" there were substituted "six months"; and

(b) subsection (2) applies as if for "51 weeks" there were substituted "one month".

11 Uniform

The appropriate national authority shall determine the uniform for traffic officers designated by, or under an authorisation given by, that authority.

12 Power to charge for traffic officer services provided on request

The appropriate national authority may, at the request of any person, agree to arrange for the services of a traffic officer to be provided to that person subject to the payment of a charge.

13 Power to acquire land

In the Highways Act 1980 (c. 66), after section 245 (acquisition of land for buildings etc. required for discharge of functions of highway authority) there is inserted—

"245A Acquisition of land by Secretary of State or Assembly for buildings etc. needed for traffic management purposes

(1) The Secretary of State may acquire land which in his opinion is required for the provision of any buildings or facilities which are needed—

(a) for use by, or in connection with the activities of, traffic officers in England; or

(b) for other purposes connected with the management of traffic on highways in England for which he is the highway authority.

(2) The National Assembly for Wales may acquire land which in its opinion is required for the provision of any buildings or facilities which are needed—

(a) for use by, or in connection with the activities of, traffic officers in Wales; or

(b) for other purposes connected with the management of traffic on highways in Wales for which it is the highway authority."

14 Financial assistance to authorised persons

The appropriate national authority may give financial assistance to an authorised person, in such form and on such terms as it considers appropriate, in respect of the traffic officers designated by that person (including financial assistance in respect of equipment, accommodation or other facilities provided for those traffic officers).

15 Interpretation of Part 1

In this Part—

"the appropriate national authority" means—

(a) the Secretary of State, as respects England; and

(b) the Assembly, as respects Wales;

"the Assembly" means the National Assembly for Wales;

"authorised person" means a person who is authorised under section 2;

"designation" means designation as a traffic officer under section 2;

"relevant road" has the meaning given by section 1(5);

"road" means any length of highway or of any other road to which the public has access, and includes bridges over which a road passes;

"traffic authority" has same meaning as in the Road Traffic Regulation Act 1984 (c. 27);

"traffic officer" means an individual designated under section 2.

PART 2

NETWORK MANAGEMENT BY LOCAL TRAFFIC AUTHORITIES

General duties relating to network management

16 The network management duty

(1) It is the duty of a local traffic authority to manage their road network with a view to achieving, so far as may be reasonably practicable having regard to their other obligations, policies and objectives, the following objectives—

(a) securing the expeditious movement of traffic on the authority's road network; and

(b) facilitating the expeditious movement of traffic on road networks for which another authority is the traffic authority.

(2) The action which the authority may take in performing that duty includes, in particular, any action which they consider will contribute to securing—

(a) the more efficient use of their road network; or

(b) the avoidance, elimination or reduction of road congestion or other disruption to the movement of traffic on their road network or a road network for which another authority is the traffic authority;

and may involve the exercise of any power to regulate or co-ordinate the uses made of any road (or part of a road) in the road network (whether or not the power was conferred on them in their capacity as a traffic authority).

(3) In this Part "network management duty", in relation to a local traffic authority, means their duty under this section.

17 Arrangements for network management

(1) A local traffic authority shall make such arrangements as they consider appropriate for planning and carrying out the action to be taken in performing the network management duty.

(2) The arrangements must include provision for the appointment of a person (to be known as the "traffic manager") to perform such tasks as the authority consider will assist them to perform their network management duty.

(3) The traffic manager may (but need not) be an employee of the authority.

(4) The arrangements must include provision for establishing processes for ensuring (so far as may be reasonably practicable) that the authority—

(a) identify things (including future occurrences) which are causing, or which have the potential to cause, road congestion or other disruption to the movement of traffic on their road network; and

(b) consider any possible action that could be taken in response to (or in anticipation of) anything so identified;

but nothing in this subsection is to be taken to require the identification or consideration of anything appearing to have only an insignificant effect (or potential effect) on the movement of traffic on their road network.

(5) The arrangements must include provision for ensuring that the authority—

(a) determine specific policies or objectives in relation to different roads or classes of road in their road network;

(b) monitor the effectiveness of—

(i) the authority's organisation and decision-making processes; and

(ii) the implementation of their decisions; and

(c) assess their performance in managing their road network.

(6) The authority must keep under review the effectiveness of the arrangements they have in place under this section.

18 Guidance to local traffic authorities

(1) The appropriate national authority may publish guidance to local traffic authorities about the techniques of network management or any other matter relating to the performance of the duties imposed by sections 16 and 17.

(2) In performing those duties a local traffic authority shall have regard to any such guidance.

19 Power to require information relating to network management

(1) The appropriate national authority may direct a local traffic authority to provide it, within a specified period, with specified information connected with any aspect of the performance of their duties under sections 16 and 17.

(2) The information that may be specified in such a direction—

(a) must be information which the authority have in their possession or can reasonably be expected to acquire; and

(b) includes, in particular, information relating to—

(i) the management of a local traffic authority's road network; or

(ii) the use of their road network by different kinds of traffic or the effects of that use.

(3) A direction under this section may be given to two or more local traffic authorities or to local traffic authorities of a description specified in the direction.

(4) A direction under this section given to a London authority must be copied to the Mayor.

Enforcement of network management duties

20 Intervention notices

(1) If the appropriate national authority considers that a local traffic authority may be failing properly to perform any of their duties under sections 16 and 17 it may give a notice stating that it is of that opinion (an "intervention notice") to the authority.

(2) An intervention notice must—

(a) give brief particulars of the grounds for giving the notice; and

(b) offer the local traffic authority the opportunity (within a specified period) to make representations or proposals about any matter raised by the notice.

(3) The notice may also require the local traffic authority to provide the national authority, within the period specified under subsection (2)(b), with specified information.

(4) Any information specified in the notice must be information that the national authority considers will assist it in deciding what further action (if any) to take.

(5) The Secretary of State shall consult the Mayor before giving an intervention notice to a London authority and, if such a notice is given, shall give him a copy of it.

21 Intervention orders

(1) If the appropriate national authority is satisfied that a local traffic authority are failing properly to perform any duty under sections 16 and 17 it may, by order made by statutory instrument (an "intervention order"), make provision for or in connection with the appointment of a traffic director.

(2) In this Part "traffic director" means a person appointed by the national authority with such objectives as the national authority considers will secure that the duty in question is properly performed.

(3) An intervention order providing for the appointment of a traffic director must (among other things)—

(a) state that the national authority is satisfied as mentioned in subsection (1);

(b) give brief particulars of the grounds for appointing a traffic director;

(c) set out the objectives of the traffic director; and

(d) confer such general powers on the traffic director as the national authority considers appropriate for achieving those objectives.

(4) But such an order may not be made unless—

(a) reasonable notice of the grounds for appointing a traffic director has been given to the local traffic authority in an intervention notice; and

(b) the period specified in the notice under section 20(2)(b) has expired;

but if that period has expired an order may be made whether or not the local traffic authority have complied with any requirements specified under section 20(3).

(5) The general powers which may be conferred on the traffic director are powers authorising him—

(a) to monitor any matter;

(b) to report on any matter;

(c) to intervene in activities of the local traffic authority; and

(d) to carry out functions of the local traffic authority.

The general powers are explained further in sections 23 to 25.

(6) The order may require the traffic director to carry out functions of the local traffic authority.

(7) The order may—

(a) limit the scope of any general powers conferred on the traffic director or any duty imposed under subsection (6);

(b) confer ancillary powers on the traffic director;

(c) provide for the circumstances in which any general or ancillary power may (or may not) be exercised;

(d) impose conditions on the exercise of any general or ancillary power;

(e) make incidental or supplementary provision;

(f) make different provision for different circumstances.

(8) For the purposes of subsection (7) "ancillary power" means a power to do anything calculated to facilitate (or to be conducive or incidental to)—

(a) the exercise by the traffic director of his general powers; or

(b) the performance of any duty imposed on him under subsection (6),

including, in particular, power to require the local traffic authority to provide him with information and assistance.

(9) The appropriate national authority shall consult the local traffic authority before making an intervention order which makes further provision in connection with the appointment of a traffic director under an earlier intervention order.

(10) The Secretary of State shall consult the Mayor before making an intervention order in relation to a London authority.

22 Appointment of traffic director: supplementary

(1) Where by virtue of an intervention order a traffic director is to be appointed in relation to a local traffic authority—

(a) any person (including the national authority making the order, another local traffic authority, a Passenger Transport Executive or any other public authority) may be appointed;

(b) the appointment may be made on such terms as that national authority may consider appropriate; and

(c) the appointment may be revoked by that national authority.

(2) The powers conferred by subsection (1) have effect subject to the provisions of the order.

(3) Notice of any appointment of a traffic director (or the revocation of an appointment) shall be given to the local traffic authority and, in the case of a London authority, to the Mayor.

(4) Any such notice of an appointment must be given before the traffic director begins to carry out any of his duties.

23 Monitoring and reporting

(1) The general powers which may be conferred by an intervention order under section 21(5)(a) are powers to monitor anything connected with the performance by the local traffic authority of their duties under 16 and 17, including the use of their road network by different kinds of traffic or the effects of that use.

(2) The general powers which may be conferred by an intervention order under section 21(5)(b) are powers to make reports about—

- (a) anything connected with the carrying out of the traffic director's objectives; or
- (b) anything connected with the performance by the local traffic authority of their duties under sections 16 and 17, including the use of their road network by different kinds of traffic or the effects of that use.

(3) The order may provide for such reports to be made to the appropriate national authority or the local traffic authority (or both).

24 Intervention in activities of local traffic authority

(1) This section explains the general powers which may be conferred by an intervention order under section 21(5)(c).

(2) Such powers may authorise the traffic director to give to the local traffic authority directions with respect to the exercise of any specified function, including in particular directions—

- (a) to exercise (or to cease or refrain from exercising) such a function;
- (b) as to the way in which such a function is (or is not) to be exercised;
- (c) as to the policies to be adopted in the exercise of any function.

(3) The order may specify any function of the authority (whether or not conferred in their capacity as a traffic authority) the exercise of which appears to the appropriate national authority to be capable of contributing to, or interfering with, the achievement of the traffic director's objectives.

(4) Such powers may also authorise the traffic director, where it appears to him that the authority has failed to comply with a direction—

- (a) to take any steps which still remain to be taken by the authority to comply with the direction, and
- (b) recover from the authority as a civil debt the costs reasonably incurred by him in taking those steps.

(5) Anything done by the traffic director under subsection (4)(a) is to be treated as having been done by the authority.

25 Exercise of local traffic authority functions

(1) This section explains the general powers which may be conferred by an intervention order under section 21(5)(d) and the duty which may be imposed under section 21(6).

(2) The order may authorise or require the traffic director to take over from the authority the exercise of any specified function.

(3) The order may specify any function of the authority (whether or not conferred in their capacity as a traffic authority) the exercise of which appears to the appropriate national authority to be capable of contributing to, or interfering with, the achievement of the traffic director's objectives.

(4) The order may require the authority to take action—

- (a) to co-ordinate their activities with those of the traffic director in the exercise of functions specified under subsection (2);
- (b) to co-operate with the traffic director in the exercise of such functions.

(5) Anything done by the traffic director in the exercise of a specified function is to be treated as having been done by the authority.

26 Application of sections 20 to 25 to local traffic authorities exercising functions jointly

(1) The appropriate national authority may by order made by statutory instrument make provision for the application of sections 20 to 25 (with or without modifications) in cases where to any extent the performance of the duties under sections 16 and 17 is carried out jointly by two or more local traffic authorities.

(2) A statutory instrument containing an order under this section made by the Secretary of State is subject to annulment in pursuance of a resolution by either House of Parliament.

27 Criteria for making intervention orders

(1) The appropriate national authority shall give, in accordance with subsection (2), guidance about the criteria which it proposes to apply for the purpose of deciding whether to give an intervention notice or make an intervention order.

(2) The guidance shall be appended to an order made by the authority by statutory instrument.

(3) A statutory instrument containing an order under subsection (2) made by the Secretary of State is subject to annulment in pursuance of a resolution of either House of Parliament.

28 Guidance to traffic directors

(1) The appropriate national authority may give guidance to traffic directors in relation to the performance of their duties.

(2) Such guidance may be general or given to a particular traffic director.

(3) In carrying out his duties a traffic director shall have regard to any guidance under this section which is applicable to him.

(4) The appropriate national authority shall publish any guidance given under this section.

29 Traffic directors in London

(1) Subsections (2) to (4) apply where a traffic director is appointed in relation to a London authority.

(2) A copy of any report made by a traffic director to the authority shall be given to the Mayor.

(3) In carrying out his duties the traffic director need not comply with, or have regard to, any directions or guidance given by the Mayor under Part 4 of the Greater London Authority Act 1999 (c. 29).

(4) The duty to comply with a direction given by the traffic director prevails, to the extent of any inconsistency, over the duty to comply with, or have regard to, any direction or guidance mentioned in subsection (3).

(5) Subsections (6) to (8) apply where a traffic director is appointed in relation to Transport for London.

(6) If the traffic director—

(a) exercises the power of Transport for London under subsection (3) of section 301A of the Highways Act 1980 (c. 66) to object to a proposal and does not withdraw that objection, or

(b) directs Transport for London to exercise the power to object to a proposal and not to withdraw the objection,

that section has effect as if subsections (3)(d) and (4) were omitted.

(7) If the traffic director—

(a) exercises the power of Transport for London under subsection (3) of section 121B of the Road Traffic Regulation Act 1984 (c. 27) to object to a proposal and does not withdraw that objection, or

(b) directs Transport for London to exercise the power to object to a proposal and not to withdraw the objection,

that section has effect as if subsections (3)(d) and (4) were omitted.

(8) While the intervention order to which the appointment relates is in force the Mayor may not, without the consent of the traffic director, issue a direction under—

(a) section 301A(9) of the Highways Act 1980, or

(b) section 121B(9) of the Road Traffic Regulation Act 1984,

dispensing with any of the requirements mentioned there (whether or not by varying an existing direction).

30 Recovery of costs from local traffic authorities

(1) This section applies where a traffic director has been appointed in respect of a local traffic authority.

(2) The appropriate national authority may recover from the local traffic authority such sum or sums as it may consider appropriate.

(3) The amount recovered must not exceed the total expenditure of the national authority which is attributable to the appointment of the traffic director (including expenditure towards any costs incurred by the traffic director which are not met from any other source).

31 Interpretation of Part 2

In this Part—

"appropriate national authority" means—

(a) the Secretary of State, as respects England; and

(b) the National Assembly for Wales, as respects Wales;

"intervention notice" means a notice under section 20;

"intervention order" means an order under section 21;

"local traffic authority" means a traffic authority other than the Secretary of State or the National Assembly for Wales;

"London authority" means Transport for London, a London borough Council or the Common Council of the City of London;

"Mayor" means the Mayor of London;

"road" means any length of highway or of any other road to which the public has access, and includes bridges over which a road passes;

"road network", in relation to a local traffic authority, means the network of roads for which the authority is the traffic authority;

"traffic" includes pedestrians;

"traffic authority" has the same meaning as in the Road Traffic Regulation Act 1984 (c. 27);

"network management duty" has the meaning given in section 16(3).

PART 3

PERMIT SCHEMES

32 Meaning of "permit scheme"

(1) Any reference in this Part to a permit scheme is a reference to a scheme which is designed to control the carrying out of specified works in specified streets in a specified area.

(2) A permit scheme may (in particular) include provision—

(a) for or in connection with requiring a permit to be obtained before specified works are carried out (including provision as to the persons who are required to obtain permits),

(b) for or in connection with the issue of permits (including provision with respect to applications for permits, provision for cases in which there is to be an entitlement to the issue of a permit and provision with respect to cases in which permits are to be deemed to be issued),

(c) as to cases in which specified works may be carried out without a permit,

(d) for or in connection with the imposition of conditions which are to apply in relation to the carrying out of specified works (including provision for or in connection with the attachment of such conditions to permits),

(e) for or in connection with the review or variation of permits or such conditions (including provision with respect to applications for such variations).

(3) In this section "specified" means specified, or of a description specified, in a permit scheme.

33 Preparation of permit schemes

(1) A local highway authority, or two or more such authorities acting together, may prepare and submit to the appropriate national authority a permit scheme.

(2) The appropriate national authority may direct a local highway authority, or two or more such authorities acting together, to prepare and submit to the national authority a permit scheme which takes such form as the national authority may direct.

(3) The appropriate national authority, in its capacity as a highway authority, may prepare a permit scheme.

(4) The Secretary of State, in his capacity as the person with responsibility for the management and control of streets in the Royal Parks, may prepare a permit scheme in respect of any such streets.

(5) Those preparing permit schemes—

(a) must comply with permit regulations, and

(b) must have regard to any guidance which may be issued by the appropriate national authority.

34 Implementation of local highway authority permit schemes

(1) This section applies where a permit scheme is prepared and submitted to the appropriate national authority ("the authority") in accordance with section 33(1) or (2).

(2) The authority may approve the scheme with or without modifications.

(3) Where it approves the scheme with modifications, references in subsections (4) and (5) to the scheme are to be read as references to the scheme as so modified.

(4) The scheme shall not have effect unless the authority by order gives effect to it.

(5) An order under subsection (4)—

(a) must set out the scheme and specify the date on which the scheme is to come into effect, and

(b) may (in accordance with permit regulations) include provisions which disapply or modify enactments to the extent specified in the order.

35 Implementation of other permit schemes

(1) This section applies where a permit scheme is prepared in accordance with section 33(3) or (4).

(2) The scheme shall not have effect unless the appropriate national authority by order gives effect to it.

(3) An order under subsection (2)—
 (a) must set out the scheme and specify the date on which the scheme is to come into effect, and
 (b) may (in accordance with permit regulations) include provisions which disapply or modify enactments to the extent specified in the order.

36 Variation and revocation of permit schemes

(1) The appropriate national authority may by order vary or revoke any permit scheme which for the time being has effect.

(2) An order under this section—
 (a) may relate to one or more permit schemes,
 (b) may vary or revoke any order under section 34 or 35, or any order previously made under this section,
 (c) may (in accordance with permit regulations) include provisions which disapply or modify enactments to the extent specified in the order.

37 Permit regulations

(1) The appropriate national authority may by regulations ("permit regulations") make provision with respect to the content, preparation, submission, approval, operation, variation or revocation of permit schemes.

(2) Permit regulations may—
 (a) set out procedural provisions with which those preparing permit schemes must comply,
 (b) set out standard provisions which may or must be included in a permit scheme,
 (c) make provision as to the publicity to be given to permit schemes.

(3) Permit regulations may make provision—
 (a) with respect to any of the matters mentioned in section 32(2) (including provision as to the conditions or types of conditions which may be imposed by virtue of section 32(2)(d)),
 (b) for the purpose of limiting the streets, or type of streets, which may be the subject of a permit scheme.

(4) Permit regulations may make provision—
 (a) as to the criteria to be taken into account in the case of decisions with respect to the issue, review or variation of permits or decisions with respect to the imposition, review or variation of conditions,
 (b) for or in connection with the determination, or facilitating the determination, of disputes (including provision with respect to the appointment of persons to determine, or facilitate the determination of, disputes),
 (c) for or in connection with appeals (including provision with respect to the appointment of persons to hear appeals),
 (d) as to the action which may be taken if works are carried out without a permit or if any conditions are not complied with,
 (e) for or in connection with the creation, in prescribed cases (including prescribed cases where works are carried out without a permit or in breach of

any conditions), of a criminal offence triable summarily and punishable with a fine not exceeding level 5 on the standard scale,

(f) for or in connection with excluding or limiting the liability of prescribed undertakers in prescribed cases.

(5) Provision under subsection (4) in respect of adjudication may not be made without the consent of the Lord Chancellor.

(6) Permit regulations may make provision for or in connection with the giving of fixed penalty notices (including, in particular, provision applying Schedule 4B to the New Roads and Street Works Act 1991 (c. 22), with or without modifications) in relation to any offence created by permit regulations.

(7) Permit regulations may make provision for or in connection with the payment of a fee in respect of any one or more of the following—

(a) an application for a permit,

(b) the issue of a permit,

(c) an application for the variation of a permit or the conditions attached to a permit,

(d) the variation of a permit or the conditions attached to a permit.

(8) Provision made under subsection (7) may include provision as to—

(a) the amount or maximum amount of any fee,

(b) cases in which fees are not to be payable or are to be repaid,

(c) cases in which fees may be discounted,

(d) the time and manner of making payment of fees,

(e) the application of sums paid by way of fees.

(9) In making provision under subsection (7), the appropriate national authority must try to ensure, so far as is reasonably practicable, that the fees payable in connection with permit schemes do not exceed such costs in connection with permit schemes as may be prescribed.

(10) For the purposes of subsection (9), the national authority may rely on such estimates (including estimates with respect to the average costs of highway authorities or particular descriptions of highway authority) as the national authority thinks fit.

(11) Permit regulations may make provision—

(a) for or in connection with the creation and maintenance of registers of permits,

(b) with respect to access to information contained in any such registers (including provision restricting such access),

(c) with respect to the keeping of accounts, and the preparation and publication of statements of account, relating to permit schemes.

(12) Permit regulations may make provision for or in connection with permitting a highway authority, or two or more such authorities acting together, to prepare a permit scheme in respect of streets in a particular area which are maintainable highways notwithstanding that the authority, or those authorities, are not the highway authority for all or any of those streets.

(13) Permit regulations may set out provisions—

(a) which disapply or modify enactments, and

(b) which are to or may apply in the case of permit schemes.

(14) Nothing in subsections (2) to (13) is to be taken as affecting the generality of subsection (1).

38 Crown application

(1) This Part and any provisions made under it bind the Crown (but do not affect Her Majesty in her private capacity or in right of Her Duchy of Lancaster or the Duke of Cornwall).

(2) Nothing in subsection (1) is to be construed as authorising the bringing of proceedings for a criminal offence against a person acting on behalf of the Crown.

39 Interpretation of Part 3

(1) In this Part—

"the appropriate national authority" means—

(a) the Secretary of State, as respects England, and

(b) the National Assembly for Wales, as respects Wales;

"condition" is to be construed in accordance with section 32(2);

"enactment" includes an enactment comprised in subordinate legislation (within the meaning of the Interpretation Act 1978 (c. 30));

"fixed penalty notice" means a notice offering a person the opportunity of discharging any liability to conviction for an offence by payment of a penalty;

"highway authority" and "local highway authority" have the same meaning as in the Highways Act 1980 (c. 66);

"maintainable highway" has the same meaning as in Part 3 of the New Roads and Street Works Act 1991 (c. 22);

"permit" is to be construed in accordance with section 32(2);

"permit scheme" is to be construed in accordance with section 32;

"permit regulations" is to be construed in accordance with section 37;

"prescribed" means prescribed, or of a description prescribed, by regulations made by the appropriate national authority;

"Royal Park" means any park to which the Parks Regulation Act 1872 (c. 15) applies (see sections 1 and 3 of the Parks Regulation (Amendment) Act 1926 (c. 36));

"street" means a street (within the meaning of Part 3 of the New Roads and Street Works Act 1991)—

(a) which is a maintainable highway, or

(b) which is situated in a Royal Park;

"street works" has the meaning given by section 48(3) of the New Roads and Street Works Act 1991;

"undertaker" has the same meaning as in Part 3 of that Act;

"works" means—

(a) prescribed street works, and

(b) such other works or activities as may be prescribed,

but activities may not be prescribed under paragraph (b) unless they are, or correspond to, activities which are regulated or controlled by the Highways Act 1980.

(2) An order or regulations under this Part—

(a) may make different provision for different cases or different areas,

(b) may include incidental, supplemental, consequential or transitional provision or savings.

(3) A power to make an order or regulations under this Part is exercisable by statutory instrument.

(4) The first permit regulations may not be made by the Secretary of State unless a draft of them has been laid before and approved by a resolution of each House of Parliament.

(5) Subject to that, a statutory instrument containing regulations under this Part made by the Secretary of State is subject to annulment in pursuance of a resolution of either House of Parliament.

PART 4

STREET WORKS

Enforcement

40 Increase in penalties for summary offences under 1991 Act

(1) The maximum fine for each offence under a provision of the New Roads and Street Works Act 1991 (c. 22) (in this Part referred to as "the 1991 Act") listed in column 1 of the table in Schedule 1 is increased from level 3 on the standard scale to the level specified for that provision in column 3 of the table.

(2) Accordingly, in each provision so listed, for "level 3" there is substituted "level 4" or "level 5" (as specified in column 3 of the table).

(3) In section 70(6) of the 1991 Act, for the words from "to a" to the end there is substituted—

"(a) in the case of an offence consisting of a failure to comply with subsection (3) or (4A), to a fine not exceeding level 4 on the standard scale; and

(b) in any other case, to a fine not exceeding level 5 on that scale."

(4) In section 74(7B) and 74A(11) of the 1991 Act (maximum fine for offences in regulations in respect of failure to comply with notice requirement) for "level 3" there is substituted "level 4".

(5) In section 88(6) of the 1991 Act (failure to comply with duties relating to street works affecting the structure of a bridge) for the words from "to a" to the end there is substituted—

"(a) in the case of an offence consisting of a failure to take all reasonably practicable steps to comply with subsection (5)(a), to a fine not exceeding level 4 on the standard scale; and

(b) in any other case, to a fine not exceeding level 5 on that scale."

41 Fixed penalty offences

(1) After section 95 of the 1991 Act (offences) there is inserted—

"95A Fixed penalties for certain offences under this Part

(1) Any offence under this Part relating to any street works which is listed in the first column of Schedule 4A (and described in general terms in the second column) is a fixed penalty offence for the purposes of this Part.

(2) Offences listed in that Schedule which are committed by virtue of section 166 (offences by bodies corporate and Scottish partnerships) are not fixed penalty offences.

(3) The Secretary of State may by order modify that Schedule so as to provide for offences under this Part relating to any street works to become (or cease to be) fixed penalty offences.

(4) Such an order may not be made unless a draft of the order has been laid before and approved by resolution of each House of Parliament.

(5) Schedule 4B (which makes provision about fixed penalties for fixed penalty offences) has effect."

(2) In section 106 of that Act (index for Part 3), the following entry is inserted in the appropriate place—

"fixed penalty offence	section 95A(1)".

(3) After Schedule 4 to that Act there is inserted Schedules 4A and 4B as set out in Schedules 2 and 3 to this Act.

Co-ordination of works by street authority

42 Duty of street authority to co-ordinate works

(1) Section 59 of the 1991 Act (general duty of street authority to co-ordinate works) is amended as follows.

(2) In subsection (1) after "purposes)" there is inserted "and the carrying out of relevant activities".

(3) In subsection (2) after "works" there is inserted "or relevant activities".

(4) After subsection (6) there is inserted—

"(7) In this section "relevant activities" means any activity, other than the execution of works in the street or the use of the street by traffic (including pedestrians), which—

(a) involves the temporary occupation or use of space in a street;

(b) is subject to regulation by the street authority by virtue of provision made by or under any Act other than this Act; and

(c) is prescribed by regulations made by the Secretary of State."

Direction-making powers

43 Directions relating to timing of street works

(1) Section 56 of the 1991 Act (power to give directions as to timing of street works) is amended as follows.

(2) In subsection (1)—

(a) in paragraph (b), after "at certain times" there is inserted "or on certain days (or at certain times on certain days)";

(b) after "the times" there is inserted "or days (or both)".

(3) After subsection (1) there is inserted—

"(1A) Where it appears to a street authority—

(a) that subsisting street works are causing or are likely to cause serious disruption to traffic, and

(b) that the disruption would be avoided or reduced if the works were to continue to be carried out only at certain times or on certain days (or at certain times on certain days),

the authority may give the undertaker such directions as may be appropriate as to the times or days (or both) when the works may or may not continue to be carried out."

(4) After subsection (3) there is inserted—

"(3A) An undertaker shall be taken not to have failed to fulfil any statutory duty to afford a supply or service if, or to the extent that, his failure is attributable to a direction under this section."

44 Directions as to placing of apparatus

In the 1991 Act, after section 56 there is inserted—

"56A Power to give directions as to placing of apparatus

(1) Where—

(a) an undertaker is proposing to execute street works consisting of the placing of apparatus in a street ("street A"),

(b) placing the apparatus in street A is likely to cause disruption to traffic, and

(c) it appears to the street authority that—

(i) there is another street ("street B") in which the apparatus could be placed, and

(ii) the conditions in subsection (2) are satisfied,

the authority may by direction require the undertaker not to place the apparatus in street A (but may not require him to place the apparatus in street B).

(2) The conditions referred to in subsection (1)(c) are that—

(a) disruption to traffic would be avoided or reduced if the apparatus were to be placed in street B;

(b) placing the apparatus in street B would be a reasonable way of achieving the purpose for which the apparatus is to be placed; and

(c) it is reasonable to require the undertaker not to place the apparatus in street A.

(3) A direction under this section may be varied or revoked by a further such direction.

(4) The procedure for giving a direction under this section shall be prescribed by the Secretary of State.

(5) The Secretary of State may by regulations make provision for appeals against directions under this section, including provision as to the persons who may determine appeals and the procedure to be followed on an appeal.

(6) An undertaker who executes works in contravention of a direction under this section commits an offence and is liable on summary conviction to a fine not exceeding level 5 on the standard scale.

(7) An undertaker shall be taken not to have failed to fulfil any statutory duty to afford a supply or service if, or to the extent that, his failure is attributable to a direction under this section.

(8) The Secretary of State may issue or approve for the purposes of this section a code of practice giving practical guidance as to the exercise by street authorities of the power conferred by this section; and in exercising that power a street authority shall have regard to the code of practice."

Records and information

45 The street works register

(1) Section 53 of the 1991 Act (the street works register) is amended as follows.

(2) In subsection (1)—

(a) after "respect to" (in the second place they appear) there is inserted "(a)"; and

(b) at the end there is added "; and

(b) such descriptions of—

(i) apparatus placed, or proposed to be placed, in the street,

(ii) builder's skips (within the meaning of section 139 of the Highways Act 1980 (c. 66))), or of building materials, rubbish or other things deposited, or proposed to be deposited, in the street; or

(iii) scaffolding or other structures which are erected, or proposed to be erected, in the street,

as may be prescribed."

(3) After subsection (4) there is inserted—

"(4A) In subsection (4) "central register" means a register covering the areas of two or more street authorities."

(4) After subsection (5) there is inserted—

"(5A) In particular the Secretary of State may require a street authority to share information in their possession with a person appointed to keep a central register which discharges the duties of that authority under this section."

46 Records of location of apparatus

(1) Section 79 of the 1991 Act (records of location of apparatus) is amended as follows.

(2) After subsection (1) there is inserted—

"(1A) An undertaker may, except in such cases as may be prescribed, include in his records under subsection (1) a record of the location of any item of apparatus belonging to him which is not required to be so included, stating the nature of the apparatus and (if known) whether it is for the time being in use."

(3) After subsection (2) there is inserted—

"(2A) Regulations under subsection (2) which alter the form or manner in which the records are to be kept may apply to records made before (as well as records made after) the alterations take effect."

(4) After subsection (3) there is inserted—

"(3A) In subsections (2) to (3) the references to an undertaker's records are to the records kept by him under subsection (1) (including anything included in those records by virtue of any provision of this Act or any other enactment)."

47 Duties relating to the location of unexpected apparatus

(1) Section 80 of the 1991 Act (duties where person finds unidentified apparatus) is amended as follows.

(2) In subsection (1) for "made available by the undertaker" there is substituted "kept by the undertaker under section 79(1) and made available by him".

(3) After subsection (1) there is inserted—

"(1A) Subsection (1) has effect subject to such exceptions as may be prescribed."

(4) For subsections (2) and (3) there is substituted—

"(2) Where a person executing works of any description in the street finds apparatus which does not belong to him and is unable, after taking such steps as are reasonably practicable, to ascertain to whom the apparatus belongs, he shall comply with such requirements (if any) as may be prescribed for the purpose of securing that he—

(a) makes and keeps a record of the location of the apparatus and (so far as appears from external inspection) its nature and whether it is in use; and

(b) informs the street authority or any other person of those matters.

(2A) Regulations under subsection (2) may make provision—

(a) as to the form and manner in which records are to be kept;

(b) as to the form and manner in which, or the time at or by which, information is to be given; and

(c) for records which are to be kept by undertakers to be included in the records kept by them under section 79(1)."

(5) In subsection (4) for "(2)" there is substituted "any requirement imposed on him by regulations under subsection (2)".

(6) After subsection (4) there is added—

"(5) The Secretary of State may by regulations make provision for and in connection with the keeping (whether by the Secretary of State or a person with whom he has made appropriate arrangements) of a register of information recorded by undertakers in pursuance of a requirement imposed under subsection (2).

(6) Regulations under subsection (5) may make provision about the inspection of the register by any person having authority to execute works of any description in the street or otherwise appearing to the person responsible for keeping the register to have a sufficient interest."

48 Duty to inspect records

After section 53 of the 1991 Act (the street works register) there is inserted—

"53A Duty to inspect records

(1) The Secretary of State may make provision by regulations requiring an undertaker proposing to execute street works of a prescribed description to inspect prescribed statutory records before commencing the street works.

(2) The regulations may provide for the manner in which an inspection of any statutory records is to be carried out.

(3) The regulations may prescribe evidence which may be relied on by the undertaker to demonstrate that he has carried out an inspection required by the regulations.

(4) The regulations may in particular require the undertaker—

(a) to be in possession of prescribed evidence before commencing the street works; and

(b) to produce, in such manner as may be prescribed, prescribed evidence to the street authority either at the request of the authority or at or by such time as may be prescribed.

(5) The regulations may provide for the cases or circumstances in which a requirement under subsection (1) or (4) does or does not apply.

(6) The regulations may create a summary offence, punishable with a fine not exceeding level 5 on the standard scale, in respect of any contravention by an undertaker of a requirement of the regulations.

(7) In this section "statutory record" means any register or other record kept in pursuance of a requirement imposed by—

(a) an enactment; or

(b) a licence or other instrument having effect under or by virtue of an enactment."

Miscellaneous

49 Notices of street works

(1) In section 54 of the 1991 Act (advance notice of certain works)—

(a) in subsection (3) for "contain such" there is substituted "state the date on which it is proposed to begin the works and shall contain such other";

(b) after subsection (4) there is inserted—

"(4A) If an undertaker who has given advance notice under this section has not, before the starting date specified in the notice, given to the street authority a notice under section 55 in respect of the works, he shall within such period as may be prescribed give to that authority a notice containing such information as may be prescribed.

(4B) An advance notice under this section shall cease to have effect in relation to the proposed works (so that subsection (1) applies again in relation to the works) if those works are not substantially begun before the end of such period beginning with the starting date specified in the notice as may be prescribed, or such further period as the street authority may allow.

(4C) Different periods may be prescribed under subsection (4B) for different descriptions of works."

(2) In section 55 of that Act (notice of starting date of works) after subsection (7) there is inserted—

"(8) If a notice under this section ceases to have effect the undertaker shall, within such period as may be prescribed, give a notice containing such information as may be prescribed to those to whom the notice under this section was required to be given.

(9) An undertaker who fails to give notice in accordance with subsection (8) commits an offence and is liable on summary conviction to a fine not exceeding level 4 on the standard scale."

(3) In section 93 of that Act (works affecting level crossings or tramways) in subsection (2) for "(7)" there is substituted "(9)".

50 Qualifications of supervisors and operatives

(1) Section 67 of the 1991 Act (qualifications of supervisors and operatives) is amended as follows.

(2) After subsection (1) there is inserted—

"(1A) A street authority may (unless the case is one excepted from subsection (1)) by notice require an undertaker executing street works—

(a) to notify them of the name of—

(i) the person who is currently the qualified supervisor required by subsection (1); and

(ii) each person who has previously been the qualified supervisor so required; and

(b) to provide them with such evidence of the requisite qualification of each person named as may be prescribed."

(3) After subsection (2) there is inserted—

"(2A) A street authority may (unless the case is one excepted from subsection (2)) by notice require an undertaker executing street works—

(a) to notify them of the name of—

(i) a person whose presence on site at any time specified in the notice (being a time when the works were in progress) enabled the undertaker to comply with his duty under subsection (2); or

(ii) each person whose presence on site during the progress of the works enabled the undertaker to comply with his duty in subsection (2); and

(b) to provide them with such evidence of the requisite qualification of each person named as may be prescribed.

(2B) A notice under subsection (1A) or (2A) may be given at any time while the works are being executed or within such period after their completion as may be prescribed.

(2C) The undertaker shall comply with a notice under subsection (1A) or (2A) within such period as may be prescribed."

(4) In subsection (3) for "or (2)" there is substituted ", (2) or (2C)".

(5) In subsection (4), after paragraph (b) there is inserted "and

(c) the form of any document to be issued by an approved body to certify or otherwise show that a qualification has been conferred on any person."

51 Restriction on works following substantial road works

(1) Section 58 of the 1991 Act (restriction on works following substantial road works) is amended as specified in subsections (2) to (8).

(2) In subsection (1), for the words "twelve months" there is substituted "prescribed period".

(3) In subsection (2), after "prescribed" there is inserted "form and" and for "three months" there is substituted "such period as may be prescribed".

(4) In subsection (3) after paragraph (e) there is inserted "and

(f) any other person of a prescribed description;"

(and the word "and" after paragraph (d) is omitted).

(5) In subsection (4), for paragraphs (a) and (b) there is substituted "within such period as may be prescribed".

(6) In subsection (6), at the beginning of paragraph (b) there is inserted "if he is convicted of an offence under this subsection".

(7) In subsection (7), for "by arbitration" there is substituted "in the prescribed manner".

(8) After that subsection there is inserted—

"(7A) Regulations under subsection (7) may in particular make provision for the question referred to in that subsection to be settled—

(a) by arbitration;

(b) by a person designated by the Secretary of State on appeal by the undertaker."

(9) In section 55 of the 1991 Act (notice of starting date of works), in subsection (2), after "works," there is inserted "or in cases where the undertaker has been given notice under section 58(1),".

52 Restriction on works following substantial street works

(1) After section 58 of the 1991 Act there is inserted—

"58A Restriction on works following substantial street works

Schedule 3A shall have effect."

(2) After Schedule 3 to that Act there is inserted Schedule 3A as set out in Schedule 4 to this Act.

(3) In section 57 of that Act (notice of emergency works)—

(a) in subsection (1) after "works)" there is inserted "or paragraph 2(1)(d) or 3(1) of Schedule 3A (notification of proposed works or directions as to timings of works)";

(b) in subsection (2) after "is" there is inserted "(or would, but for paragraph 2(6) of Schedule 3A, be)".

(4) In section 64 of that Act (traffic-sensitive streets) in subsection (1) after "works)" there is inserted "or paragraph 2 of Schedule 3A".

(5) In section 74 of that Act (charge for occupation of highway where works unreasonably prolonged)in subsection (3)(b) after "date)" there is inserted "or notification under paragraph 2(1)(d) of Schedule 3A (notification of proposed works)".

(6) In section 88 of that Act (provisions relating to bridges)in subsection (4) after "date)" there is inserted ", or making a notification under paragraph 2(1)(d) of Schedule 3A (notification of proposed works),".

(7) In section 89 of that Act (provisions relating to sewers)in subsection (2) after "date)" there is inserted ", or making a notification under paragraph 2(1)(d) of Schedule 3A (notification of proposed works),".

53 Notices requiring remedial works relating to reinstatements

(1) In section 72 of the 1991 Act (powers of street authority in relation to reinstatement)—

(a) in subsection (3), for "of not less than 7 working days" there is substituted ", not being less than such period as may be prescribed,"; and

(b) after subsection (3) there is inserted—

"(3A) Different minimum periods may be prescribed under subsection (3) for different descriptions of remedial works; and cases may be prescribed in which no minimum period applies."

(2) In section 90 of the 1991 Act (powers of street authority in relation to reinstatement of sewers, etc.)—

(a) in subsection (2), for "of not less than 7 working days" there is substituted ", not being less than such period as may be prescribed,"; and

(b) after subsection (2) there is inserted—

"(2A) Different minimum periods may be prescribed under subsection (2) for different descriptions of remedial works; and cases may be prescribed in which no minimum period applies."

54 Duty to notify street authority of reinstatement

(1) Section 70 of the 1991 Act (duty of undertaker to reinstate) is amended as follows.

(2) After subsection (1) there is inserted—

"(1A) The reinstatement required by subsection (1) may be permanent or interim."

(3) For subsections (3) and (4) there is substituted—

"(3) He shall within 7 working days from the date on which the reinstatement is completed give notice to the street authority of that completion—

(a) stating whether the reinstatement is permanent or interim; and

(b) giving such other information about the reinstatement as may be prescribed.

(4) If the reinstatement is interim, he shall complete the permanent reinstatement of the street as soon as reasonably practicable, and in any event within 6 months from the date on which the interim reinstatement was completed.

(4A) He shall, within 7 working days from the date on which the permanent reinstatement required by subsection (4) is completed, give notice to the street authority of that completion, giving such other information about the reinstatement as may be prescribed.

(4B) The Secretary of State may by regulations modify the period specified in subsection (3), (4) or (4A)."

55 Power of street authority to require undertaker to re-surface street

(1) After section 73 of the 1991 Act there is inserted—

"Re-surfacing

73A Power to require undertaker to re-surface street

(1) In prescribed circumstances, the street authority for a street may by notice (a "re-surfacing notice") require an undertaker within subsection (2) to execute such re-surfacing works in the street as may be specified in the notice.

(2) An undertaker is within this subsection if—

(a) he has given notice under section 54 or 55 of, or made a notification under paragraph 2(1)(d) of Schedule 3A in respect of, proposed street works,

(b) he is executing street works, or

(c) he has, within such period ending with the giving of the notice as may be prescribed (or if no period is prescribed, at any time), executed street works,

and the works will involve, involve or (as the case may be) involved the breaking up of any part of the street.

(3) The works specified in the re-surfacing notice may relate to any part of the street (including any part not, and not to be, broken up by the undertaker); but regulations may restrict the extent of the works that may be so specified.

(4) The re-surfacing notice relieves the undertaker to the extent (if any) specified in the notice of his duty under section 70 to reinstate the surface of the street; but regulations may restrict the circumstances in which and the extent to which undertakers may be relieved of that duty.

(5) The street authority may by notice to the undertaker vary or withdraw a re-surfacing notice; but regulations may restrict the circumstances in which notices may be varied or withdrawn.

(6) A street authority may give a re-surfacing notice notwithstanding that the authority (in any capacity) are under a duty to undertake any of the works specified in the notice.

(7) In this Part—

"re-surfacing notice" has the meaning given by subsection (1);

"re-surfacing works" means any works relating to the replacement of the surface of any part of a street;

"surface" includes a paved surface.

(8) The reference in subsection (2)(c) to the execution of street works is a reference to the execution of such works after the commencement of this section (whether or not regulations under it have been made).

73B Power to specify timing etc. of re-surfacing

(1) A re-surfacing notice may require an undertaker to—

(a) execute the works specified in the notice in stages so specified;

(b) begin the execution of those works (or any stage of them) at or by a date and time so specified;

(c) execute those works (or any stage of them) at times or on days (or at times on days) so specified;

(d) complete the execution of those works (or any stage of them) by a date and time so specified.

(2) The Secretary of State may by regulations make provision restricting, in some or all cases, the power to include requirements within subsection (1), including provision that—

(a) requires a street authority to consult an undertaker before a prescribed description of requirement is included in a notice;

(b) provides that any date specified in a notice for the beginning, execution or completion of works shall not be earlier than a prescribed period from the date on which the notice is given.

73C Materials, workmanship and standard of re-surfacing

(1) An undertaker who has been given a re-surfacing notice shall, when executing the works specified in the notice, comply with such requirements as may be prescribed as to the specification of materials to be used and the standards of workmanship to be observed.

(2) He shall also ensure that the new surface conforms to such performance standards as may be prescribed, for the prescribed period after completion of the works."

(2) In section 106 of that Act—

(a) after the entry for relevant authority (in relation to street works) there is inserted—

"re-surfacing notice	section 73A(7)
re-surfacing works	section 73A(7)";

(b) after the entry for street works licence there is inserted—

"surface	section 73A(7)".

56 Re-surfacing: regulations and guidance

After section 73C of the 1991 Act there is inserted—

"73D Re-surfacing: regulations

(1) The Secretary of State may make regulations supplementing sections 73A to 73C.

(2) The regulations may in particular—

(a) make provision about the information to be contained in a re-surfacing notice (including the way in which re-surfacing works are to be described);

(b) prescribe, for cases where a re-surfacing notice may be given to more than one undertaker, the matters that a street authority shall take into account when selecting the undertaker to whom the notice is to be given;

(c) impose a requirement on an undertaker, in prescribed circumstances, to give notice to the street authority of a prescribed event;

(d) prescribe circumstances in which an undertaker may elect to make a payment to the street authority instead of executing the works specified in a re-surfacing notice, and make provision about the calculation of the amount of such payments;

(e) confer a right of review or appeal against a re-surfacing notice or any requirement contained in it, and may make provision about the period within which and manner in which any such right may be exercised and about the determination of appeals and the persons who may determine them;

(f) require disputes of a prescribed description (including disputes as to the existence of circumstances prescribed under section 73A(1)) to be determined in such manner and by such persons as may be prescribed;

(g) apply any provisions of this Part or the Highways Act 1980 (c. 66), with or without modifications, in relation to works specified in a re-surfacing notice (and provide that for those purposes the works are to be treated as street works or works of any other description).

(3) The regulations may provide that where a re-surfacing notice has been served on an undertaker, the street authority may (in such circumstances and to such extent as may be prescribed) by notice relieve any other undertaker within section 73A(2) of his duty under section 70 to reinstate the surface of the street.

(4) The regulations may create in respect of any breach of a requirement imposed by a re-surfacing notice or of the duty imposed by section 73C, or any contravention of the regulations, an offence punishable on summary conviction—

(a) where the offence consists of a failure to give a notice in accordance with the regulations, with a fine not exceeding level 4 on the standard scale;

(b) in any other case, with a fine not exceeding level 5 on the standard scale.

(5) The first regulations under this section or any of sections 73A to 73C shall not be made unless a draft of them has been laid before and approved by a resolution of each House of Parliament; subsequent regulations shall be subject to annulment in pursuance of a resolution of either House of Parliament.

73E Re-surfacing: guidance

(1) The Secretary of State may, for the purposes of sections 73A to 73D (including regulations under those sections), issue or approve a code of practice giving practical guidance as to the exercise of powers and the discharge of duties under those sections.

(2) In exercising those powers and in discharging those duties, street authorities and undertakers shall have regard to the code of practice."

57 Contributions to costs of re-surfacing by undertaker

(1) After section 78 of the 1991 Act there is inserted—

"78A Contributions to costs of re-surfacing by undertaker

(1) Where a street authority has given a re-surfacing notice to an undertaker (A)—

(a) the authority shall pay to A a proportion, calculated in the prescribed manner, of the costs reasonably incurred by A in executing the works specified in the notice;

(b) an undertaker to whom subsection (2) applies shall pay to A a proportion, calculated in the prescribed manner, of those costs.

(2) This subsection applies to an undertaker if—

(a) he has, after the commencement of this section (whether or not regulations under it have been made) and before the completion of the works specified in the notice, executed street works which involved the breaking up of any part of a street, and

(b) the works specified in the notice include the re-surfacing of that part of the street.

(3) The Secretary of State may by regulations prescribe exceptions to the duty imposed by subsection (1)(b).

(4) The payments referred to in subsection (1) shall be made in such instalments and manner, and within such period of such event, as may be prescribed.

(5) The Secretary of State may by regulations make provision—

(a) requiring a street authority, within such period of such event as may be prescribed, to give to an undertaker to whom subsection (2) applies a notice containing such information as may be prescribed;

(b) requiring a street authority to pay to an undertaker to whom it has given a re-surfacing notice such sum as he has been unable to recover under subsection (1)(b) on account of the insolvency of an undertaker;

(c) requiring disputes of a prescribed description (including disputes as to whether subsection (2) applies to an undertaker) to be determined in such manner and by such persons as may be prescribed.

(6) For the purposes of this section, any costs incurred by an undertaker (including any costs of a street authority which are borne by the undertaker) in consequence of a failure by the undertaker to comply with any duty under this Part shall be treated as having been incurred unreasonably.

(7) The Secretary of State may by regulations make provision requiring undertakers to make payments to a street authority where—

(a) the authority has given a re-surfacing notice to an undertaker,

(b) that undertaker has exercised a right, conferred by regulations under section 73D, of the sort mentioned in subsection (2)(d) of that section, and

(c) the authority has carried out any of the works specified in the notice.

(8) The power in subsection (7) includes power to make provision corresponding to provision that may be made under subsections (1) to (5).

(9) Regulations under this section may make different provision for cases where an undertaker mentioned in subsection (1) or (7) has made, or is liable to make, a payment under section 78.

(10) The first regulations under this section shall not be made unless a draft of them has been laid before and approved by a resolution of each House of

Parliament; subsequent regulations shall be subject to annulment in pursuance of a resolution of either House of Parliament.

(11) In subsection (5)(b) "insolvency"—

(a) in relation to a company, has the meaning given by section 247(1) of the Insolvency Act 1986;

(b) in relation to an individual, includes the approval of a voluntary arrangement under Part 8 of that Act."

(2) In section 96 of the 1991 Act, in subsection (3), after "street)" there is inserted "or 78A (contributions to costs of re-surfacing by undertakers)".

58 Inspection fees

(1) In section 72 of the 1991 Act (powers of street authority in relation to reinstatement) after subsection (2) there is inserted—

"(2A) The Secretary of State may prescribe a fee in respect of a prescribed description of inspection mentioned in subsection (2).

If he does so that subsection has effect, in relation to that description of inspection, as if for "he shall bear the cost of" there were substituted "he shall pay the prescribed fee in respect of".

(2B) The power to make different provision under subsection (2A) for different cases includes power—

(a) to make different provision for different descriptions of street authority or undertakers;

(b) to prescribe different fees by reference to the nature or extent of the inspection, the place where it is carried out and such other factors as appear to the Secretary of State to be relevant."

(2) For section 75 of that Act (inspection fees) there is substituted—

"75 Inspection fees

(1) The Secretary of State may make provision by regulations requiring an undertaker to pay to the street authority the prescribed fee in respect of—

(a) all inspections carried out by the authority of his street works; or

(b) such inspections of those works as may be prescribed.

(2) The regulations may—

(a) require undertakers to make payments in respect of inspections anticipated to take place within a prescribed period; and

(b) make provision for the striking of an account between an undertaker and a street authority and the making of any necessary payment or repayment.

(3) The power to make different provision under this section for different cases includes power—

(a) to make different provision for different descriptions of street authority or different descriptions of undertakers (including descriptions framed by reference to their previous performance);

(b) to prescribe different fees by reference to the nature or extent of the excavation or other works, the place where they are executed and such other factors as appear to the Secretary of State to be relevant.

(4) The reference in subsection (3)(a) to the previous performance of an undertaker is to the performance of the undertaker, during such period as may be prescribed, as respects such description of his duties under this Part as may be prescribed.

(5) The regulations may require disputes of any prescribed description to be determined by arbitration.

(6) Nothing in this section applies to inspections in respect of which the undertaker is obliged to bear the cost, or pay the prescribed fee, under section 72(2) (inspections consequent on failure to comply with duties as to reinstatement)."

59 Guidance about inspections

After section 73E of the 1991 Act (as inserted by section 56 above) there is inserted—

"Inspections

73F Guidance about street authority inspections

(1) The Secretary of State may issue or approve guidance to street authorities about any matter relating to the exercise by them of any power to carry out inspections of street works.

(2) In exercising their powers to carry out such inspections a street authority shall have regard to any guidance issued or approved under this section.

(3) In this section any reference to inspections includes the carrying out of investigatory works."

PART 5

HIGHWAYS AND ROADS

Strategic roads in London

60 Strategic roads in London: initial designation by Secretary of State

(1) The Secretary of State may by order made by statutory instrument designate roads and proposed roads in Greater London, other than roads for which the Secretary of State or Transport for London is the traffic authority, as strategic roads for the purposes of—

(a) section 301A of the 1980 Act, and

(b) section 121B of the 1984 Act.

(2) Any road or proposed road so designated shall become a strategic road as from such date as may be specified in the order.

(3) No order under subsection (1) may be made in respect of a road or proposed road in a London borough if an order under that subsection has been made in respect of any other road or proposed road in that borough.

(4) In this section and section 61—

(a) "road" means any length of highway or of any other road to which the public has access, and includes bridges over which a road passes;

(b) "strategic road" means a road which is for the time being a strategic road by virtue of an order under subsection (1) or section 61(1);

(c) "traffic authority" has the same meaning as in the 1984 Act.

(5) For the purposes of this section and section 61—

(a) the City of London shall be treated as if it were a London borough;

(b) the Common Council shall be treated as if it were the council for a London borough;

(c) the Inner Temple and the Middle Temple shall be treated as forming part of the City.

(6) In this Part—

"the 1980 Act" means the Highways Act 1980 (c. 66);

"the 1984 Act" means the Road Traffic Regulation Act 1984 (c. 27).

(7) A statutory instrument containing an order under this section is subject to annulment in pursuance of a resolution of either House of Parliament.

61 Orders of the Greater London Authority changing what are strategic roads

(1) If the Mayor of London considers it expedient that any road or proposed road in Greater London, other than a road for which the Secretary of State or Transport for London is the traffic authority, should become a strategic road then the Greater London Authority may by order direct that the road or proposed road shall become a strategic road.

(2) Subject to subsection (3), an order under subsection (1) takes effect on such date as may be specified in the order.

(3) An order under subsection (1) is of no effect unless—

(a) it is made with the consent of the council for the London borough in which the road is situated (or proposed road is to be situated), or

(b) if that consent is refused, it is confirmed (with or without modifications) by the Secretary of State.

(4) If the Mayor considers it expedient that any strategic road should cease to be such a road then the Greater London Authority may by order direct that the road shall cease to be such a road.

(5) An order under subsection (4) takes effect on such date as may be specified in the order.

(6) The functions of the Greater London Authority under this section are functions exercisable by the Mayor acting on its behalf.

(7) Section 124C of the 1984 Act (certification and records) applies in relation to strategic roads as it applies in relation to GLA side roads.

62 London borough council exercising powers under Highways Act 1980 so as to affect strategic roads

(1) Section 301A of the 1980 Act (London borough council exercising powers under that Act so as to affect certain roads) is amended as follows.

(2) In subsection (1)—

(a) at the end of paragraph (a) there is inserted—

"(aa) a strategic road,";

(b) in paragraph (b), after "borough" there is inserted "other than a GLA road or strategic road".

(3) In subsection (3)(a), for the words from "by Transport for London" to the end there is substituted "—

(i) in the case of a GLA road, by Transport for London;

(ii) in the case of a strategic road, by Transport for London and, where the road concerned is in another London borough, the council for that borough;

(iii) in the case of a road within subsection (1)(b), by the London borough council concerned; or".

(4) After subsection (3) there is inserted—

"(3A) References in paragraphs (b) to (d) of subsection (3) to objections are to objections made by a person who, in the circumstances, has the power to give an approval under paragraph (a) of that subsection."

(5) In subsection (5)(a), for the words from "a GLA road" to the end there is substituted "—

(i) a GLA road,

(ii) a strategic road, or

(iii) a road in another London borough other than a GLA road or strategic road, and".

(6) In subsection (10)—

(a) in paragraph (b), at the end there is inserted "or strategic roads";

(b) in paragraph (c), for "neither GLA roads nor" there is substituted "not GLA roads, strategic roads or".

(7) After subsection (16) there is inserted—

"(17) In this section "strategic road" has the meaning given by section 60 of the Traffic Management Act 2004."

63 London borough council exercising powers under Road Traffic Regulation Act 1984 so as to affect strategic roads

(1) Section 121B of the 1984 Act (London borough council exercising powers under that Act so as to affect certain roads) is amended as follows.

(2) In subsection (1)—

(a) at the end of paragraph (a) there is inserted—

"(aa) a strategic road,";

(b) in paragraph (b), after "borough" there is inserted "other than a GLA road or strategic road".

(3) In subsection (3)(a), for the words from "by Transport for London" to the end there is substituted "—

(i) in the case of a GLA road, by Transport for London;

(ii) in the case of a strategic road, by Transport for London and, where the road concerned is in another London borough, the council for that borough;

(iii) in the case of a road within subsection (1)(b), by the London borough council concerned; or".

(4) After subsection (3) there is inserted—

"(3A) References in paragraphs (b) to (d) of subsection (3) to objections are to objections made by a person who, in the circumstances, has the power to give an approval under paragraph (a) of that subsection."

(5) In subsection (5)(a), for the words from "a GLA road" to the end there is substituted "—

(i) a GLA road,

(ii) a strategic road, or

(iii) a road in another London borough other than a GLA road or strategic road, and".

(6) In subsection (10)—

(a) in paragraph (b), at the end there is inserted "or strategic roads";

(b) in paragraph (c), for "neither GLA roads nor" there is substituted "not GLA roads, strategic roads or".

(7) After subsection (12) there is inserted—

"(13) In this section "strategic road" has the meaning given by section 60 of the Traffic Management Act 2004."

Enforcement of certain offences under the Highways Act 1980

64 Fixed penalty offences under the Highways Act 1980

(1) After section 314 of the 1980 Act (offences by body corporate) there is inserted—

"314A Fixed penalties for certain offences under Part 9

(1) A fixed penalty offence is any offence under Part 9 which—

(a) is listed in the first column in Schedule 22A (and described in general terms in the second column), and

(b) is prescribed in regulations made by the Secretary of State.

(2) Offences listed in that Schedule which are committed by virtue of section 314 (offences committed by bodies corporate, etc.) are not fixed penalty offences.

(3) Schedule 22B (which makes provision about fixed penalties for fixed penalty offences) has effect.

(4) Regulations under subsection (1)(b) may—

(a) make provision for Greater London different from that made for the rest of England;

(b) make consequential provision (including provision disapplying sections 8 to 11 of, and Schedule 2 to, the London Local Authorities and Transport for London Act 2003 in relation to any offence prescribed in such regulations);

(c) make transitional provision."

(2) In section 322(5) of that Act (service of notices etc.), after paragraph (a) there is inserted—

"(ab) a notice under Schedule 22B to this Act;".

(3) After Schedule 22 to that Act there is inserted Schedules 22A and 22B as set out in Schedules 5 and 6 to this Act.

(4) In the New Roads and Street Works Act 1991 (c. 22), in section 97 (service of notices etc.) after subsection (2) there is inserted—

"(3) References in this section to notices authorised to be given or served for the purposes of this Part include a reference to notices under Schedule 22B to the Highways Act 1980 (fixed penalties for certain offences under that Act)."

(5) In the London Local Authorities and Transport for London Act 2003 (c. iii), in section 11 (fixed penalties: reserve powers of Secretary of State) after subsection (6) there is inserted—

"(7) The Secretary of State may make regulations increasing the level of fixed penalty under this Act in respect of an offence listed in Schedule 22A to the Highways Act 1980 (as well as Schedule 4 to this Act).

(8) While regulations under subsection (7) are in force in respect of an offence, the borough councils and Transport for London may not set the level of fixed penalty in respect of that offence below that set by the regulations."

Records of objects placed in highway

65 Duty of local highway authority to keep records of objects in highway

(1) The appropriate national authority may by regulations made by statutory instrument require a local highway authority to make and keep a record of the location of any object of a description specified in the regulations which has been placed by that authority in a street.

(2) Regulations under this section may include provision—

(a) as to the form in which a record is to be made;

(b) as to supplementary information to be included in a record;

(c) requiring a record to be made available for inspection.

(3) The reference in subsection (1) to an object placed in a street includes an object placed under, over, across, along or upon a street.

(4) In this section—

"appropriate national authority" means—

(a) the Secretary of State, in relation to local highway authorities in England;

(b) the National Assembly for Wales, in relation to local highway authorities in Wales;

"street" has the same meaning as in Part 3 of the New Roads and Street Works Act 1991.

(5) A statutory instrument containing regulations under this section made by the Secretary of State is subject to annulment in pursuance of a resolution of either House of Parliament.

Skips, scaffolding, building materials and excavations: charges for occupation of highway etc.

66 Builders' skips: charge for occupation of highway for unreasonable period

For section 140A of the 1980 Act there is substituted—

"140A Builders' skips: charge for occupation of highway for unreasonable period

(1) The Secretary of State may make provision by regulations requiring the owner of a builder's skip deposited on a highway maintainable at the public expense to pay a charge to the highway authority where the period for which the skip remains in the highway exceeds—

(a) such period as may be prescribed, and

(b) a reasonable period.

(2) For this purpose "a reasonable period" means such period as is agreed by the authority and the owner of the skip to be reasonable or, in default of such agreement, is determined by arbitration to be reasonable in the circumstances.

(3) In default of agreement, the authority's view as to what is a reasonable period shall be acted upon pending the decision of the arbitrator.

(4) The regulations may prescribe exemptions from the requirement to pay charges.

(5) The regulations may provide—

(a) that in prescribed circumstances (including in particular where any person makes an application for permission under section 139) the owner of the skip shall give to the authority, in such manner and within such period as may be prescribed, notice containing an estimate of the likely duration of the occupation of the highway, and

(b) that the period stated in the notice shall be taken to be agreed by the authority to be reasonable unless the authority give notice, in such manner and within such period as may be prescribed, objecting to the estimate.

(6) The regulations may also provide—

(a) that in prescribed circumstances the owner of the skip shall give to the authority, in such manner and within such period as may be prescribed, notice containing a revised estimate of the likely duration of the occupation of the highway, and

(b) that upon the notice being given any previous agreement to or determination of a reasonable period ceases to have effect, and the period stated in the notice shall be taken to be agreed by the authority to be reasonable unless the authority give notice, in such manner and within such period as may be prescribed, objecting to the revised estimate.

(7) The amount of the charge shall be determined in such manner as may be prescribed by reference to the period for which the highway is occupied by the skip.

(8) The regulations may prescribe different rates of charge according to—

(a) the extent to which the skip occupies the highway;

(b) the place and time of the occupation;

(c) such other factors as appear to the Secretary of State to be relevant.

(9) The regulations may provide—

(a) that the authority are to set the rate of charge, up to a prescribed maximum, and

(b) that different rates of charge may be set according to such factors as the authority consider relevant.

(10) The regulations may make provision for the determination of the duration of the occupation of the highway for the purposes of the regulations.

(11) And they may, in particular, make provision for an occupation to be treated as beginning or ending on the giving of, or as stated in, a notice given by the owner of the skip to the authority, in the prescribed manner, in accordance with a requirement imposed by the regulations.

(12) The regulations may make provision requiring the owner of the skip to provide the authority, in such manner and within such period as may be prescribed, with such information as the authority may specify in a notice to that person, being information required for the purposes of—

(a) determining whether a charge is payable by him;

(b) calculating the amount of any charge payable by him.

(13) The regulations may make provision as to the time and manner of making payment of charges.

(14) The regulations shall provide that a highway authority may reduce the amount, or waive payment, of a charge—

(a) in any particular case,

(b) in such classes of case as they may decide or as may be prescribed, or

(c) in all cases or in all cases other than a particular case or such class of case as they may decide or as may be prescribed.

(15) The regulations may make provision as to—

(a) the application by local highway authorities of sums paid by way of charges, and

(b) the keeping of accounts, and the preparation and publication of statements of account, relating to sums paid by way of charges.

(16) The regulations may create in respect of any failure to give a notice, or to provide information, required by the regulations a criminal offence triable summarily and punishable with a fine not exceeding level 4 on the standard scale.

(17) The regulations may provide that where a skip is the subject of a prescribed description of hiring agreement or hire purchase agreement, the person in possession of the skip under the agreement is for the purposes of the regulations to be treated as the owner of the skip.

(18) The regulations may make provision about their application to a series of deposits of skips.

(19) And they may, in particular, provide that a series of deposits of skips is to be treated as a single deposit of a skip—

(a) beginning at the time the first in the series was deposited, and

(b) ending at the time the last in the series was removed.

(20) In this section—

"builder's skip" has the meaning given by section 139(11);

"prescribed" means prescribed by the Secretary of State by regulations, which may make different provision for different cases."

67 Builders' skips: charge determined by reference to duration of occupation of highway

After section 140A of the 1980 Act there is inserted—

"140B Builders' skips: charge determined by reference to duration of occupation of highway

(1) The Secretary of State may make provision by regulations requiring the owner of a builder's skip deposited on a highway maintainable at the public expense to pay to the highway authority a charge determined, in the prescribed manner, by reference to the period for which the highway is occupied by the skip.

(2) The regulations shall not require charges to be paid to a local highway authority unless the Secretary of State has, by order, approved the authority for the purposes of the regulations.

(3) The regulations may require disputes of any prescribed description to be referred to an arbitrator appointed in accordance with the regulations.

(4) Subsections (4) and (8) to (20) of section 140A apply in relation to regulations under subsection (1) of this section as they apply in relation to regulations under subsection (1) of that section."

68 Scaffolding, building materials and excavations: charge for occupation of highway for unreasonable period

For section 171A of the 1980 Act there is substituted—

"171A Scaffolding, building materials and excavations: charge for occupation of highway for unreasonable period

(1) The Secretary of State may make provision by regulations requiring a person who—

(a) erects a relevant structure on or over a highway maintainable at the public expense,

(b) deposits building materials, rubbish or other things in such a highway, or

(c) makes a temporary excavation in such a highway,

to pay a charge to the highway authority in the circumstances set out in subsection (3).

(2) The reference in subsection (1)(a) to the erection of a relevant structure is a reference to the erection, in connection with any building or demolition work or the alteration, repair, maintenance or cleaning of any building, of any scaffolding or other structure that obstructs the highway.

(3) The circumstances are that the period (in this section, the "relevant period") for which—

(a) a relevant structure is on or over the highway,

(b) things are deposited in the highway, or (as the case may be)

(c) there is an excavation in the highway,

exceeds both the prescribed period and a reasonable period.

(4) For this purpose "a reasonable period" means such period as is agreed by the authority and the person to be reasonable or, in default of such agreement, is determined by arbitration to be reasonable in the circumstances.

(5) In default of agreement, the authority's view as to what is a reasonable period shall be acted upon pending the decision of the arbitrator.

(6) The regulations may prescribe exemptions from the requirement to pay charges.

(7) The regulations may provide—

(a) that in prescribed circumstances (including in particular where an application is made for a licence under section 169 or consent under section 171) a person who intends to do or who does an activity mentioned in subsection (1)(a) to (c) shall give to the authority, in such manner and within such period as may be prescribed, notice containing an estimate of the likely duration of the relevant period, and

(b) that the period stated in the notice shall be taken to be agreed by the authority to be reasonable unless the authority give notice, in such manner and within such period as may be prescribed, objecting to the estimate.

(8) The regulations may also provide—

(a) that in prescribed circumstances a person who has given a notice of a type mentioned in subsection (7) shall give to the authority, in such manner and within such period as may be prescribed, notice containing a revised estimate of the likely duration of the relevant period, and

(b) that upon the notice being given any previous agreement to or determination of a reasonable period ceases to have effect, and the period stated in the notice shall be taken to be agreed by the authority to be reasonable unless the authority give notice, in such manner and within such period as may be prescribed, objecting to the revised estimate.

(9) The amount of the charge shall be determined in such manner as may be prescribed by reference to the relevant period.

(10) The regulations may prescribe different rates of charge according to—

(a) the extent to which the highway is affected by the structure, things deposited or excavation;

(b) the place and time at which the highway is so affected;

(c) such other factors as appear to the Secretary of State to be relevant.

(11) The regulations may provide—

(a) that the authority are to set the rate of charge, up to a prescribed maximum, and

(b) that different rates of charge may be set according to such factors as the authority consider relevant.

(12) The regulations may make provision for the determination of the duration of the relevant period for the purposes of the regulations.

(13) And they may, in particular, make provision for the relevant period to be treated as beginning or ending on the giving of, or as stated in, a notice given by the person mentioned in subsection (1) to the authority, in the prescribed manner, in accordance with a requirement imposed by the regulations.

(14) The regulations may make provision requiring a person who does an activity mentioned in subsection (1)(a) to (c) to provide the authority, in such manner and within such period as may be prescribed, with such information as the authority may specify in a notice to that person, being information required for the purposes of—

(a) determining whether a charge is payable by him;

(b) calculating the amount of any charge payable by him.

(15) The regulations may make provision as to the time and manner of making payment of charges.

(16) The regulations shall provide that a highway authority may reduce the amount, or waive payment, of a charge—

(a) in any particular case,

(b) in such classes of case as they may decide or as may be prescribed, or

(c) in all cases or in all cases other than a particular case or such class of case as they may decide or as may be prescribed.

(17) The regulations may make provision as to—

(a) the application by local highway authorities of sums paid by way of charges, and

(b) the keeping of accounts, and the preparation and publication of statements of account, relating to sums paid by way of charges.

(18) The regulations may create in respect of any failure to give a notice, or to provide information, required by the regulations a criminal offence triable summarily and punishable with a fine not exceeding level 4 on the standard scale.

(19) The regulations may make provision about their application to a series of deposits of things.

(20) And they may, in particular, provide that a series of deposits of things is to be treated as a single deposit of things—

(a) beginning at the time the first in the series was deposited, and

(b) ending at the time the last in the series was removed.

(21) The regulations may make provision corresponding to that mentioned in subsections (19) and (20) in relation to the erection of relevant structures and the making of excavations.

(22) In this section "prescribed" means prescribed by the Secretary of State by regulations, which may make different provision for different cases."

69 Scaffolding, building materials and excavations: charge determined by reference to duration of occupation of highway

After section 171A of the 1980 Act there is inserted—

"171B Scaffolding, building materials and excavations: charge determined by reference to duration of occupation of highway

(1) The Secretary of State may make provision by regulations requiring a person who—

(a) erects a relevant structure on or over a highway maintainable at the public expense,

(b) deposits building materials, rubbish or other things in such a highway, or

(c) makes a temporary excavation in such a highway,

to pay a charge to the highway authority.

(2) The reference in subsection (1)(a) to the erection of a relevant structure is a reference to the erection, in connection with any building or demolition work or the alteration, repair, maintenance or cleaning of any building, of any scaffolding or other structure that obstructs the highway.

(3) The charge shall be determined in the prescribed manner, by reference to the period (in this section, the "relevant period") for which—

(a) a relevant structure is on or over the highway,

(b) things are deposited in the highway, or (as the case may be)

(c) there is an excavation in the highway.

(4) The regulations shall not require charges to be paid to a local highway authority unless the Secretary of State has, by order, approved the authority for the purposes of the regulations.

(5) The regulations may require disputes of any prescribed description to be referred to an arbitrator appointed in accordance with the regulations.

(6) Subsections (6) and (10) to (22) of section 171A apply in relation to regulations under subsection (1) of this section as they apply in relation to regulations under subsection (1) of that section."

70 Sections 66 to 69: supplementary

(1) In section 139 of the 1980 Act, in subsection (11) for ", section 140 and section 140A" there is substituted "and section 140".

(2) After section 140B of that Act there is inserted—

"140C Regulations under sections 140A and 140B

Nothing shall be taken to prevent the imposition of charges by both regulations under section 140A and regulations under section 140B in respect of the same builder's skip at the same time."

(3) After section 171B of that Act there is inserted—

"171C Regulations under sections 171A and 171B

Nothing shall be taken to prevent the imposition of charges by both regulations under section 171A and regulations under section 171B in respect of the same structure, things or excavation at the same time."

(4) In section 325 of that Act (provisions as to regulations), in subsection (2A)—

(a) in paragraph (a), after "140A" there is inserted "or 140B";

(b) for paragraphs (b) and (c) there is substituted—

"(b) the first regulations for the purposes of section 171A or 171B as they apply in relation to the erection of relevant structures, or

(c) the first regulations for the purposes of section 171A or 171B as they apply in relation to the deposit of building materials, rubbish or other things and the making of temporary excavations,".

Guidance as to safety precautions

71 Guidance to local highway authorities as to safety precautions

In section 174 of the 1980 Act (precautions to be taken by persons executing works in streets), after subsection (1) there is inserted—

"(1A) The Secretary of State may give guidance to local highway authorities as to the discharge by them of their obligations under subsection (1)(a) and (b) where they are executing works for road purposes.

(1B) A local highway authority must in executing any works for road purposes have regard to any guidance given under subsection (1A).

(1C) In subsections (1A) and (1B) "works for road purposes" has the same meaning as in Part 3 of the New Roads and Street Works Act 1991."

PART 6

CIVIL ENFORCEMENT OF TRAFFIC CONTRAVENTIONS

Civil penalties for road traffic contraventions

72 Civil penalties for road traffic contraventions

(1) The appropriate national authority may make provision by regulations for or in connection with—

(a) the imposition of penalty charges in respect of road traffic contraventions that—

(i) are subject to civil enforcement (see section 73), and

(ii) are committed in an area that is a civil enforcement area for contraventions of that description (see section 74), and

(b) the payment of such penalty charges.

(2) The regulations shall include provision specifying the person or persons by whom a penalty charge in respect of a contravention is to be paid (who may be the owner of the vehicle involved in the contravention, its driver at the time of the contravention or any other appropriate person).

(3) The regulations shall include provision in respect of any description of conduct for which a penalty charge may be imposed—

(a) prohibiting criminal proceedings or the issuing of a fixed penalty notice in respect of conduct of that description, or

(b) securing that a penalty charge is not required to be paid, or is refunded, where the conduct is the subject of criminal proceedings or of a fixed penalty notice.

(4) The regulations may include provision prohibiting the imposition of a penalty charge except on the basis of—

(a) a record produced by an approved device, or

(b) information given by a civil enforcement officer as to conduct observed by him.

(5) The regulations may—

(a) specify exemptions from penalty charges, and

(b) make provision for discounts or surcharges, or both.

73 Contraventions subject to civil enforcement

(1) Schedule 7 specifies the road traffic contraventions that are subject to civil enforcement.

(2) These are—

(a) parking contraventions (see Part 1 of the Schedule);

(b) bus lane contraventions (see Part 2 of the Schedule);

(c) London lorry ban contraventions (see Part 3 of the Schedule);
(d) moving traffic contraventions (see Part 4 of the Schedule).

(3) Regulations under this Part of this Act may make different provision in relation to different descriptions of contravention.

(4) The appropriate national authority may by regulations make such consequential amendment of Schedule 7 as appears to the authority to be required in consequence of the amendment, replacement or revocation of any provision of subordinate legislation referred to in that Schedule.

74 Civil enforcement areas

(1) Schedule 8 makes provision—
(a) as to the areas that are civil enforcement areas for the purposes of different descriptions of road traffic contravention, and
(b) as to the meaning of "enforcement authority" in relation to road traffic contraventions committed in a civil enforcement area.

(2) In that Schedule—
Part 1 makes provision for Greater London, and
Part 2 makes provision for the rest of England and Wales.

75 Power to require authority to apply for civil enforcement powers

(1) The appropriate national authority may by notice in writing under this section (a "notice to apply") require a local authority to make an application under paragraph 8 of Schedule 8 for an order designating the whole or part of the local authority's area as a civil enforcement area for parking contraventions.

(2) The notice must specify—
(a) the date by which the local authority is to make the application ("the application date"),
(b) the latest date by which the application must request that the order comes into force ("the in-force date"), and
(c) the area in respect of which the application is to be made.

(3) Before giving a notice to apply the appropriate national authority must inform the local authority concerned and the appropriate chief officer of police, in writing, of its intention to give such a notice, indicating the application date, the in-force date and the area it intends to specify in the notice.

(4) The local authority may make representations to the appropriate national authority to the effect—
(a) that a notice to apply should not be given to the authority, or
(b) that the notice should specify a different application date, a different in-force date, or a different area in respect of which the application is to be made.

(5) In considering whether to give a notice to apply the appropriate national authority must have regard to the local authority's representations and take into account—
(a) the administrative burden of creating or extending a civil enforcement area and of enforcing parking contraventions within such an area,

(b) the financial circumstances of the local authority concerned and the likely expenses and receipts in connection with the proposed civil enforcement area,

(c) any representations made by the appropriate chief officer of police, and

(d) any other factors appearing to the appropriate national authority to be relevant.

(6) After a notice to apply has been given, it may be modified by agreement between the appropriate national authority and the local authority concerned.

76 Civil enforcement officers

(1) A local authority may provide for the enforcement of road traffic contraventions for which it is the enforcement authority by individuals to be known as civil enforcement officers.

(2) A civil enforcement officer must be—

(a) an individual employed by the authority, or

(b) where the authority have made arrangements with any person for the purposes of this section, an individual employed by that person to act as a civil enforcement officer.

(3) Civil enforcement officers—

(a) when exercising specified functions must wear such uniform as may be determined by the enforcement authority in accordance with guidelines issued by the appropriate national authority, and

(b) must not exercise any of those functions when not in uniform.

(4) In subsection (3)(a) "specified" means specified by regulations made by the appropriate national authority.

(5) A parking attendant appointed under section 63A of the Road Traffic Regulation Act 1984 (c. 27) by a local authority that is an enforcement authority—

(a) is a civil enforcement officer in relation to parking contraventions for which that authority is the enforcement authority, and

(b) may be appointed a civil enforcement officer in relation to other road traffic contraventions for which they are the enforcement authority.

77 Setting the level of penalty charges

(1) Schedule 9 provides for the setting of the levels of penalty charges and certain other charges.

(2) In that Schedule—

Part 1 specifies the charges to which the Schedule applies,

Part 2 provides for charges applicable in Greater London, and

Part 3 provides for charges applicable outside Greater London.

Notification, adjudication and enforcement

78 Notification of penalty charge

(1) The Lord Chancellor may make regulations for and in connection with the notification of penalty charges.

(2) The regulations may provide for notification of a penalty charge to be given in respect of a stationary vehicle—

(a) by a notice affixed to the vehicle,

(b) by a notice given to a person appearing to be in charge of the vehicle, or

(c) in such other manner as may be specified by the regulations.

(3) The regulations may provide for notification of a penalty charge otherwise than in respect of a stationary vehicle to be given in such manner as may be specified by the regulations.

(4) The regulations may not confer power to stop vehicles.

(5) The regulations may provide that, if it appears to the enforcement authority that both the operator of a vehicle and the person in control of the vehicle are liable to a penalty charge, they may give notice to the operator requiring him to provide them with the name and address of the person who was in control of the vehicle at the time of the alleged contravention.

(6) The regulations may include provision creating criminal offences to be triable summarily and punishable with a fine not exceeding level 5 on the standard scale or such lower amount as may be specified.

79 Immobilisation of vehicle where penalty charge payable

(1) The appropriate national authority may make provision by regulations for or in connection with—

(a) the fixing of an immobilisation device to a stationary vehicle found in any place where there is reason to believe the vehicle has been permitted to remain at rest there in circumstances in which a penalty charge has become payable, and

(b) the release of the vehicle from the device only on payment of—

(i) the penalty charge mentioned in paragraph (a),

(ii) such unpaid earlier penalty charges relating to the vehicle as may be specified in the regulations, and

(iii) the charge payable in respect of the release.

(2) The regulations may make provision authorising—

(a) the fixing of an immobilisation device to the vehicle while it remains in the place where it was found, or

(b) the moving of the vehicle to another place and the fixing of an immobilisation device to it in that other place,

and providing for any power of removal that was exercisable in relation to the vehicle before it was so moved to continue to be exercisable in relation to the vehicle while it remains in the place to which it was so moved.

(3) The regulations may provide—

(a) that on any occasion when an immobilisation device is fixed to a vehicle in accordance with the regulations, the person fixing the device shall also fix to the vehicle a notice—

(i) indicating that such a device has been fixed to the vehicle and warning that no attempt should be made to drive it or otherwise put it in motion unless it has been released from the device;

(ii) specifying the steps to be taken in order to secure its release; and

(iii) giving such other information as may be specified by the regulations; and

(b) that a notice fixed to a vehicle in accordance with the regulations shall not be removed or interfered with except by or under the authority of—

(i) the owner or person in charge of the vehicle, or

(ii) the enforcement authority,

and that a person contravening that prohibition commits an offence and is liable on summary conviction to a fine not exceeding level 2 on the standard scale.

(4) The regulations may also provide—

(a) that a vehicle to which an immobilisation device has been fixed in accordance with the regulations may only be released from the device by or under the direction of a person authorised by the enforcement authority; and

(b) that a person who, without being authorised to do so in accordance with the regulations, removes or attempts to remove an immobilisation device fixed to a vehicle in accordance with the regulations commits an offence and is liable on summary conviction to a fine not exceeding level 3 on the standard scale.

(5) The regulations shall provide—

(a) that an immobilisation device must not be fixed to a vehicle if a current disabled person's badge is displayed on the vehicle; and

(b) that if, in a case in which an immobilisation device would have been fixed to a vehicle but for paragraph (a), the vehicle was not being used—

(i) in accordance with regulations under section 21 of the Chronically Sick and Disabled Persons Act 1970 (c. 44), and

(ii) in circumstances falling within section 117(1)(b) of the Road Traffic Regulation Act 1984 (c. 27) (use where a disabled person's concession would be available),

the person in charge of the vehicle commits an offence and is liable on summary conviction to a fine not exceeding level 3 on the standard scale.

(6) The regulations shall also provide that an immobilisation device must not be fixed to a vehicle in a parking place in respect of a contravention consisting of, or arising out of, a failure—

(a) to pay a parking charge with respect to the vehicle,

(b) properly to display a ticket or parking device, or

(c) to remove the vehicle from the parking space by the end of a period for which the appropriate charge was paid,

until 15 minutes have elapsed since the giving of a notification of a penalty charge in respect of the contravention.

(7) In this section—

"disabled person's badge" has the same meaning as in section 142(1) of the Road Traffic Regulation Act 1984;

"parking device" means a parking device within the meaning of section 35(3B) or 51(4) of that Act; and

"parking place" means—

(a) a parking place designated by an order under section 45 of that Act, or

(b) an off-street parking place provided under section 32(1)(a) or 57(1)(b), or under a letting or arrangement made under section 33(4), of that Act.

80 Representations and appeals

(1) The Lord Chancellor may make provision by regulations entitling a person—

(a) who is or may be liable to pay a penalty charge, or

(b) who secures the release of a vehicle from an immobilisation device on payment of an amount in accordance with regulations under section 79,

to make representations to the enforcement authority and to appeal to an adjudicator if his representations are not accepted.

(2) The regulations may make such provision in connection with the rights conferred as appears to the Lord Chancellor to be appropriate, and may in particular make provision—

(a) requiring the authority to give a person notice of the rights conferred by the regulations,

(b) as to the grounds on which, and time within which, representations may be made,

(c) requiring supporting evidence in such circumstances as may be specified,

(d) as to the duties of the authority when representations are received,

(e) as to the circumstances in which there is a right of appeal to an adjudicator,

(f) generally as to the making, determination and effect of, and procedure in connection with, appeals, and

(g) enabling an adjudicator to review any decision made on, or in the course of, an appeal.

(3) The regulations may provide that, as respects a ground on which representations may be made, the adjudicator's function on an appeal is to decide whether to direct the enforcement authority to consider or re-consider (as the case may be) any representations relating to that ground.

(4) The regulations may include provision—

(a) authorising an adjudicator to require a person—

(i) to attend to give evidence at the hearing of an appeal, and

(ii) to produce any documents in his custody or under his control relating to any matter relevant for the purposes of the appeal, and

(b) making it a criminal offence triable summarily and punishable with a fine not exceeding level 2 on the standard scale to fail to comply with such a requirement.

(5) The regulations may provide that a person who makes a representation that is false in a material particular, and does so recklessly or knowing it to be false, commits an offence triable summarily and punishable with a fine not exceeding level 5 on the standard scale.

(6) The regulations may include provision authorising an adjudicator to make an order for the payment of costs and expenses by a party to an appeal in such circumstances as may be specified.

81 Adjudicators

(1) The Lord Chancellor may make provision by regulations for and in connection with the appointment of adjudicators for the purposes of this Part.

(2) The following provisions apply in relation to the office of adjudicator—

(a) to be qualified for appointment as an adjudicator, a person must have a 5-year general qualification (within the meaning of section 71 of the Courts and Legal Services Act 1990 (c. 41));

(b) an adjudicator is appointed for a term, not exceeding five years, specified in his instrument of appointment;

(c) on the expiry of a term of appointment an adjudicator is eligible for re-appointment;

(d) an adjudicator may be removed from office only for misconduct or on the ground that he is unable or unfit to discharge his functions, but otherwise holds and vacates office in accordance with the terms of his appointment.

(3) The regulations shall provide—

(a) for adjudicators to be appointed by the relevant enforcement authorities on such terms as those authorities may decide, and

(b) for the consent of the Lord Chancellor to be required for any decision by those authorities—

(i) to appoint a person as an adjudicator,

(ii) not to re-appoint a person as an adjudicator, or

(iii) to remove a person from his office as adjudicator.

(4) The relevant enforcement authorities shall—

(a) provide, or make arrangements for the provision of, accommodation and administrative staff and facilities for adjudicators, and

(b) determine the places where adjudicators are to sit,

and shall defray all the expenses of the adjudication process and, in particular, expenses in relation to the remuneration of adjudicators.

(5) The regulations shall provide—

(a) for each adjudicator to make an annual report to the relevant enforcement authorities in accordance with such requirements as may be imposed by those authorities, and

(b) for those authorities to make and publish an annual report to the appropriate national authority on the discharge by the adjudicators of their functions.

(6) In this section "the relevant enforcement authorities" means the authorities who are enforcement authorities for the purposes of this Part in relation to road traffic contraventions (of any description).

(7) The regulations may provide for the functions of the relevant enforcement authorities under this section—

(a) to be discharged separately for Greater London, England (outside Greater London) and Wales;

(b) to be discharged by means of arrangements under section 101 of the Local Government Act 1972 (c. 70) (arrangements for discharge of functions by local authorities) or in such other way as the regulations may provide.

(8) The regulations may make provision—

(a) for treating adjudicators appointed before the commencement of this Part under section 73 of the Road Traffic Act 1991 (c. 40), or under regulations made under section 144 of the Transport Act 2000 (c. 38), as if they had been appointed under this section;

(b) for continuing in force for the purposes of this section any arrangements in force immediately before the commencement of this Part for the discharge of functions corresponding to the functions of relevant enforcement authorities under this section.

(9) The expenses of the relevant enforcement authorities under this section shall be defrayed by them in such proportions—

(a) as they may decide, or

(b) in default of a decision by them, as may be determined in accordance with regulations made—

(i) by the Secretary of State, or

(ii) if the functions of those authorities are discharged separately for Wales, by the appropriate national authority.

(10) Regulations under subsection (9)(b) may, in particular, provide—

(a) for the matter to be determined by an arbitrator appointed by a body specified in the regulations, and

(b) for the giving of directions by the Secretary of State or, as the case may be, the appropriate national authority in order to secure that the matter is referred to arbitration.

82 Enforcement of penalty charges

(1) The Lord Chancellor may make regulations for or in connection with the enforcement of penalty charges.

(2) The regulations may include provision—

(a) creating criminal offences to be triable summarily and punishable with a fine not exceeding level 5 on the standard scale or such lower amount as may be specified;

(b) for amounts payable under or by virtue of any provision of this Part to be recoverable, if a county court so orders, as if they were payable under a county court order.

An amount to which paragraph (b) applies that is so recoverable is referred to below as a "traffic contravention debt".

(3) The Lord Chancellor may by order make provision—

(a) for warrants of execution in respect of traffic contravention debts, or such class or classes of traffic contravention debts as may be specified in the order, to be executed by certificated bailiffs;

(b) as to the requirements that must be satisfied before a person takes any other step of a kind specified in the order, with a view to enforcing the payment of—

(i) a traffic contravention debt, or

(ii) such class or classes of traffic contravention debts as may be so specified.

(4) Any such order may make such incidental and supplementary provision (including modifications of any enactment other than this Act) as the Lord Chancellor considers appropriate in consequence of the provision made by the order.

(5) Any order in force immediately before the commencement of this Part under section 78(2) of the Road Traffic Act 1991 (c. 40) shall have effect after that commencement as if made under the corresponding provisions of this section and shall apply in relation to the enforcement of any traffic contravention debt.

83 Certificated bailiffs

(1) For the purposes of section 82 (enforcement of penalty charges) a person is a certificated bailiff if he is authorised to act as such by a certificate signed—

- (a) by a judge assigned to a county court district, or
- (b) in such circumstances as may be specified in regulations made by the Lord Chancellor, by a district judge.

(2) The Lord Chancellor may by regulations make provision in connection with the certification of bailiffs under this section and the execution of warrants of execution by such bailiffs.

(3) The regulations may, in particular, make provision—

- (a) as to the security (if any) to be required from certificated bailiffs,
- (b) as to the fees and expenses payable with respect to execution by certificated bailiffs, and
- (c) for the suspension or cancellation of certificates issued under this section and with respect to the effect of any such suspension or cancellation.

(4) Any regulations in force immediately before the commencement of this Part under section 78(4) to (6) of the Road Traffic Act 1991 shall have effect after that commencement as if made under the corresponding provisions of this section and anything done by or in relation to any person under such regulations shall be treated, so far as may be necessary for continuing their effect, as if done under regulations made under this section.

(5) A person who is not a certificated bailiff but who purports to levy a distress as such a bailiff, and any person authorising him to levy it, shall be deemed to have committed a trespass.

Additional contraventions in special enforcement areas

84 Designation of special enforcement areas

Schedule 10 provides for the designation of areas ("special enforcement areas") where the following sections apply—

section 85 (prohibition of double parking etc.);

section 86 (prohibition of parking at dropped footways etc.).

85 Prohibition of double parking etc.

(1) In a special enforcement area a vehicle must not be parked on the carriageway in such a way that no part of the vehicle is within 50 centimetres of the edge of the carriageway.

This is subject to the following exceptions.

(2) The first exception is where the vehicle is parked wholly within a designated parking place or any other part of the carriageway where parking is specifically authorised.

A "designated parking place" means a parking place designated by order under section 6, 9, 32(1)(b) or 45 of the Road Traffic Regulation Act 1984 (c. 27).

(3) The second exception is where the vehicle is being used for fire brigade, ambulance or police purposes.

(4) The third exception is where—

- (a) the vehicle is being used for the purposes of delivering goods to, or collecting goods from, any premises, or is being loaded from or unloaded to any premises,
- (b) the delivery, collection, loading or unloading cannot reasonably be carried out in relation to those premises without the vehicle being parked as mentioned in subsection (1), and
- (c) the vehicle is so parked for no longer than is necessary and for no more than 20 minutes.

(5) The fourth exception is where—

- (a) the vehicle is being used in connection with any of the following—
  - (i) undertaking any building operation, demolition or excavation,
  - (ii) the collection of waste by a local authority,
  - (iii) removing an obstruction to traffic,
  - (iv) undertaking works in relation to a road, a traffic sign or road lighting, or
  - (v) undertaking works in relation to a sewer or water main or in relation to the supply of gas, electricity, water or communications services,
- (b) it cannot be so used without being parked as mentioned in subsection (1), and
- (c) it is so parked for no longer than is necessary.

(6) In this section "carriageway" has the meaning given by section 329(1) of the Highways Act 1980 (c. 66).

(7) References in this section to parking include waiting, but do not include stopping where—

- (a) the driver is prevented from proceeding by circumstances beyond his control or it is necessary for him to stop to avoid an accident, or
- (b) the vehicle is stopped, for no longer than is necessary, for the purpose of allowing people to board or alight from it.

(8) The prohibition in this section is enforceable as if imposed—

- (a) in Greater London, by an order under section 6 of the Road Traffic Regulation Act 1984;
- (b) elsewhere in England and Wales, by an order under section 1 of that Act.

86 Prohibition of parking at dropped footways etc.

(1) In a special enforcement area a vehicle must not be parked on the carriageway adjacent to a footway, cycle track or verge where—

(a) the footway, cycle track or verge has been lowered to meet the level of the carriageway for the purpose of—

(i) assisting pedestrians crossing the carriageway,

(ii) assisting cyclists entering or leaving the carriageway, or

(iii) assisting vehicles entering or leaving the carriageway across the footway, cycle track or verge; or

(b) the carriageway has, for a purpose within paragraph (a)(i) to (iii), been raised to meet the level of the footway, cycle track or verge.

This is subject to the following exceptions.

(2) The first exception is where the vehicle is parked wholly within a designated parking place or any other part of the carriageway where parking is specifically authorised.

A "designated parking place" means a parking place designated by order under section 6, 9, 32(1)(b) or 45 of the Road Traffic Regulation Act 1984 (c. 27).

(3) The second exception is where the vehicle is parked outside residential premises by or with the consent (but not consent given for reward) of the occupier of the premises.

This exception does not apply in the case of a shared driveway.

(4) The third exception is where the vehicle is being used for fire brigade, ambulance or police purposes.

(5) The fourth exception is where—

(a) the vehicle is being used for the purposes of delivering goods to, or collecting goods from, any premises, or is being loaded from or unloaded to any premises,

(b) the delivery, collection, loading or unloading cannot reasonably be carried out in relation to those premises without the vehicle being parked as mentioned in subsection (1), and

(c) the vehicle is so parked for no longer than is necessary and for no more than 20 minutes.

(6) The fifth exception is where—

(a) the vehicle is being used in connection with any of the following—

(i) undertaking any building operation, demolition or excavation,

(ii) the collection of waste by a local authority,

(iii) removing an obstruction to traffic,

(iv) undertaking works in relation to a road, a traffic sign or road lighting, or

(v) undertaking works in relation to a sewer or water main or in relation to the supply of gas, electricity, water or communications services,

(b) it cannot be so used without being parked as mentioned in subsection (1), and

(c) it is so parked for no longer than is necessary.

(7) In this section "carriageway", "cycle track" and "footway" have the meanings given by section 329(1) of the Highways Act 1980 (c. 66).

(8) References in this section to parking include waiting, but do not include stopping where—

(a) the driver is prevented from proceeding by circumstances beyond his control or it is necessary for him to stop to avoid an accident, or

(b) the vehicle is stopped, for no longer than is necessary, for the purpose of allowing people to board or alight from it.

(9) The prohibition in this section is enforceable as if imposed—

(a) in Greater London, by an order under section 6 of the Road Traffic Regulation Act 1984 (c. 27),

(b) elsewhere in England and Wales, by an order under section 1 of that Act.

Supplementary

87 Guidance to local authorities

(1) The appropriate national authority may publish guidance to local authorities about any matter relating to their functions in connection with the civil enforcement of traffic contraventions.

(2) In exercising those functions a local authority must have regard to any such guidance.

88 Financial provisions

(1) The appropriate national authority may make provision by regulations—

(a) requiring the keeping of accounts, and the preparation and publication of statements of account, of the income and expenditure of enforcement authorities in connection with their functions under this Part, and

(b) as to the purposes for which any surpluses may be applied.

(2) The regulations may provide—

(a) for separate accounts to be kept in respect of an authority's functions in relation to different descriptions of contravention, and

(b) for accounts to be kept in respect of an authority's income and expenditure in respect of functions under this Part and such other functions as may be specified in the regulations.

(3) The regulations may provide that section 55 of the Road Traffic Regulation Act 1984 (financial provisions relating to income and expenditure from parking places) applies in relation to income and expenditure of enforcement authorities in connection with their functions under this Part of this Act in relation to parking contraventions, subject to such modifications as may be specified in the regulations.

(4) The regulations may provide for carrying forward a surplus arising before the commencement of this Part on an account kept under—

(a) section 55 of the Road Traffic Regulation Act 1984 as modified by an order under Schedule 3 to the Road Traffic Act 1991 (c. 40) (parking contraventions),

(b) regulations under section 144 of the Transport Act 2000 (c. 38) (bus lane contraventions), or

(c) Schedule 2 to the London Local Authorities and Transport for London Act 2003 (c. iii) (London lorry ban contraventions or moving traffic contraventions).

89 Regulations and orders

(1) Regulations and orders under this Part may make provision for Greater London different from that made for the rest of England.

(2) Regulations and orders under this Part made by the Lord Chancellor may make provision for Wales different from that made for England.

(3) Regulations and orders under this Part may contain incidental, consequential or transitional provision or savings.

(4) Regulations and orders under this Part made by a Minister of the Crown or by the National Assembly for Wales shall be made by statutory instrument.

(5) Regulations under section 80 may not be made unless a draft of them has been laid before and approved by a resolution of each House of Parliament.

(6) Subject to that, a statutory instrument containing regulations or an order under this Part made by a Minister of the Crown is subject to annulment in pursuance of a resolution of either House of Parliament.

90 Application to Crown and visiting forces

(1) This Part does not apply in relation to a vehicle that—

(a) at the relevant time is used or appropriated for use for naval, military or airforce purposes, or

(b) belongs to any visiting forces (within the meaning of the Visiting Forces Act 1952 (c. 67)) or is at the relevant time used or appropriated for use by any such forces.

(2) The provisions of this Part apply to—

(a) vehicles in the public service of the Crown that are required to be registered under the Vehicle Excise and Registration Act 1994 (c. 22) (other than those exempted by subsection (1)(a) above), and

(b) persons in the public service of the Crown.

(3) This Part does not apply in relation to Crown roads within the meaning of section 131 of the Road Traffic Regulation Act 1984 (c. 27) (application of road traffic enactments to Crown roads) unless applied by order under that section.

91 Consequential amendments

Schedule 11 provides for amendments consequential on the provisions of this Part.

92 Minor definitions

(1) In this Part—

"appropriate national authority" means—

(a) as regards England, the Secretary of State, and

(b) as regards Wales, the National Assembly for Wales;

"approved device" means a device of a description specified in an order made by the appropriate national authority;

"fixed penalty notice" has the meaning given by section 52(1) of the Road Traffic Offenders Act 1988 (c. 53);

"GLA road" means—

(a) a GLA road within the meaning of the Highways Act 1980 (c. 66) (see sections 329(1) and 14D(1) of that Act), or

(b) a GLA side road within the meaning of the Road Traffic Regulation Act 1984 (c. 27) (see sections 124A(9) and 142(1) of that Act);

"immobilisation device" has the same meaning as in section 104(9) of the Road Traffic Regulation Act 1984;

"local authority" means—

(a) as regards England, a county council, a London authority, a metropolitan district council or the Council of the Isles of Scilly,

(b) as regards Wales, a county or county borough council;

"London authority" means a London local authority or Transport for London;

"London local authority" means a London borough council or the Common Council of the City of London;

"operator", in relation to a vehicle, means a person who holds an operator's licence in respect of the vehicle under section 2 of the Goods Vehicles (Licensing of Operators) Act 1995 (c. 23);

"owner", in relation to a vehicle, means the person by whom the vehicle is kept, which in the case of a vehicle registered under the Vehicle Excise and Registration Act 1994 (c. 22) is presumed (unless the contrary is proved) to be the person in whose name the vehicle is registered;

"penalty charge" means a penalty charge imposed under this Part;

"road" has the same meaning as in the Road Traffic Regulation Act 1984;

"subordinate legislation" has the same meaning as in the Interpretation Act 1978 (c. 30) (see section 21(1) of that Act);

"traffic sign" has the meaning given by section 64 of the Road Traffic Regulation Act 1984.

(2) Any reference in this Part to contravention of an order, or of provision made by or under an order, includes a failure to comply with the order or provision.

93 Index of defined expressions

In this Part the expressions listed below are defined or otherwise explained by the provisions indicated—

appropriate national authority	section 92
approved device	section 92
bus lane contravention	Part 2 of Schedule 7
civil enforcement area	Schedule 8
civil enforcement officer	Section 76
enforcement authority	Schedule 8
fixed penalty notice	section 92

GLA road	section 92
immobilisation device	section 92
local authority	section 92
London local authority	section 92
London lorry ban contravention	Part 3 of Schedule 7
moving traffic contravention	Part 4 of Schedule 7
operator	section 92
owner	section 92
parking contravention	Part 1 of Schedule 7
penalty charge	section 92
road	section 92
road traffic contravention	Schedule 7
special enforcement area	Schedule 10
subordinate legislation	section 92
traffic sign	section 92

PART 7

MISCELLANEOUS AND GENERAL

94 Power to inspect blue badges

(1) Section 21 of the Chronically Sick and Disabled Persons Act 1970 (c. 44) (badges for display on motor vehicles used by disabled persons) is amended as follows.

(2) In subsection (4B) after "a badge" there is inserted "purporting to be".

(3) After subsection (4B) there is inserted—

"(4BA) Where it appears to a constable or enforcement officer that there is displayed on any motor vehicle a badge purporting to be of a form prescribed under this section, he may require any person who—

(a) is in the vehicle, or

(b) appears to have been in, or to be about to get into, the vehicle,

to produce the badge for inspection.

(4BB) In subsection (4BA) "enforcement officer" means—

(a) a traffic warden;

(b) a civil enforcement officer (within the meaning of section 76 of the Traffic Management Act 2004);

(c) a parking attendant (within the meaning of section 63A of the Road Traffic Regulation Act 1984).

(4BC) The power conferred on an enforcement officer by subsection (4BA) is exercisable only for purposes connected with the discharge of his functions in relation to a stationary vehicle.

(4BD) A person who without reasonable excuse fails to produce a badge when required to do so under subsection (4BA) shall be guilty of an offence."

(4) In subsection (4C) after "(4B)" there is inserted "or (4BD)".

(5) In section 117 of the Road Traffic Regulation Act 1984 (c. 27) (wrongful use of disabled person's badge), in subsection (1)(a) after "badge" there is inserted "purporting to be".

95 Application of surplus income from parking places

(1) Section 55 of the Road Traffic Regulation Act 1984 (financial provisions relating to income and expenditure of local authority in connection with parking places) is amended as follows.

(2) In subsection (4), for paragraph (d) (purposes for which surplus may be applied if further off-street parking not needed) substitute—

"(d) if it appears to the local authority that the provision in their area of further off-street parking accommodation is unnecessary or undesirable, the following purposes—

(i) meeting costs incurred, whether by the local authority or by some other person, in the provision or operation of, or of facilities for, public passenger transport services,

(ii) the purposes of a highway or road improvement project in the local authority's area,

(iii) in the case of a London authority, meeting costs incurred by the authority in respect of the maintenance of roads maintained at the public expense by them,

(iv) the purposes of environmental improvement in the local authority's area,

(v) in the case of such local authorities as may be prescribed, any other purposes for which the authority may lawfully incur expenditure;"

(3) After subsection (4A) insert—

"(4B) For the purposes of subsection (4)(d)(iv) "environmental improvement" includes—

(a) the reduction of environmental pollution (as defined in the Pollution Prevention and Control Act 1999 (c. 24); see section 1(2) and (3) of that Act);

(b) improving or maintaining the appearance or amenity of—

(i) a road or land in the vicinity of a road, or

(ii) open land or water to which the general public has access; and

(c) the provision of outdoor recreational facilities available to the general public without charge.

(4C) Regulations for the purposes of subsection (4)(d)(v) above—

(a) may prescribe all local authorities, particular authorities or particular descriptions of authority,

(b) may make provision by reference to whether the authority or authorities in question have been classified for the purposes of any other enactment as falling or not falling within a particular category, and

(c) may make provision for the continued application of that provision, in prescribed cases and to such extent as may be prescribed, where an authority that is prescribed or of a prescribed description ceases to be so.".

(4) In section 100(2) of the Local Government Act 2003 (c. 26) (powers exercisable by reference to performance categories under that Act), before paragraph (a) insert—

"(za) to make regulations for the purposes of section 55(4)(d)(v) of the Road Traffic Regulation Act 1984;".

96 Wales

References in Schedule 1 to the National Assembly for Wales (Transfer of Functions) Order 1999 (S.I. 1999/672) to—

(a) the Highways Act 1980 (c. 66),

(b) the Road Traffic Regulation Act 1984 (c. 27), and

(c) the New Roads and Street Works Act 1991 (c. 22),

are to be treated as references to those Acts as amended by this Act.

97 Financial provision

(1) There shall be paid out of money provided by Parliament—

(a) any expenditure incurred by the Secretary of State in respect of—

(i) traffic officers designated under Part 1 (including expenditure relating to the provision of financial assistance under section 14 or other expenditure relating to the provision of equipment, accommodation or other facilities);

(ii) the establishment and operation of regional centres for the management of traffic on his road network;

(iii) the provision, for purposes connected with the management of traffic on his road network, of information or advice to the public;

(iv) other activities carried out for purposes connected with the management of traffic on his road network;

(b) any other expenditure incurred by the Secretary of State in consequence or by virtue of this Act;

(c) any increase attributable to this Act in the sums payable out of money so provided by virtue of any other Act.

(2) In this section references to the Secretary of State's road network are to the network of roads in England for which he is the traffic authority (within the meaning of the Road Traffic Regulation Act 1984).

98 Repeals

Schedule 12 contains repeals.

99 Commencement, transitionals and savings

(1) The preceding provisions of this Act shall come into force on such day as the Secretary of State (as respects England) or the National Assembly for Wales (as respects Wales) may appoint by order made by statutory instrument.

(2) Different days may be appointed for different purposes.

(3) For the purposes of Part 6 (civil enforcement of road traffic contraventions), and related repeals, different days may be appointed for different areas.

(4) The Secretary of State (as respects England) or the National Assembly for Wales (as respects Wales) may by order made by statutory instrument make transitional provision or savings in connection with the coming into force of any provision of this Act.

100 Short title and extent

(1) This Act may be cited as the Traffic Management Act 2004.

(2) This Act extends to England and Wales only.

Status: This is the original version (as it was originally enacted).

SCHEDULES

SCHEDULE 1

Section 40

INCREASE IN MAXIMUM FINES FOR CERTAIN SUMMARY OFFENCES UNDER THE 1991 ACT

Provision specifying fine	*Brief description of offence or offences to which the fine relates*	*New maximum fine*
Section 51(2)	Offences under s. 51(1) (prohibition of authorised street works)	level 5
Section 54(5)	Failure to comply with duties under s.54 (advance notice of certain works, etc.)	level 4
Section 55(5)	Beginning to execute works in contravention of s. 55 (notice of starting date of works)	level 4
Section 56(3)	Execution of works in contravention of direction under s. 56 (directions as to timing of street works)	level 5
Section 57(4)	Failure to give notice in accordance with s. 57 (notice of emergency works)	level 4
Section 58(6)(a)	Carrying out works in contravention of a restriction imposed under s. 58 (restriction on works following substantial road works)	level 5
Section 60(3)	Failure to comply with duty under s. 60(1) (general duty of undertakers to co-operate)	level 5
Section 65(4)	Failure to comply with s. 65(1) or (2) (safety measures)	level 5
Section 65(6)	Interference with safety measures taken by undertaker	level 5
Section 66(2)	Failure to comply with s. 66(1) (duty to carry on and complete certain street	level 5

Provision specifying fine	*Brief description of offence or offences to which the fine relates*	*New maximum fine*
	works with all reasonably practicable dispatch)	
Section 67(3)	Failure to comply with s.67(1), (2) or (2C) (duties relating to the use of qualified supervisors and operatives)	level 5
Section 68(2)	Failure by undertaker to afford street authority with reasonable facilities for ascertaining whether he is complying with his duties under Part 3	level 4
Section 69(2)	Failure to comply with s. 69(1) (requirements relating to street works likely to affect another person's apparatus in the street)	level 4
Section 71(5)	Failure to comply with duties under s. 71 (prescribed requirements as to materials and workmanship and performance standards for reinstatements)	level 5
Section 79(4)	Failure to comply with duties under s. 79(1) to (3) (records of location of apparatus)	level 5
Section 80(4)	Failure to comply with s. 80(1) (duty to inform other undertaker of location of certain apparatus) or requirements imposed under s.80(2) (duties applicable where ownership of certain apparatus cannot be ascertained)	level 4
Section 83(3)	Failure by authority to comply with s. 83(2) (requirements relating to certain road works likely to affect apparatus in the street)	level 4
Section 92(2)	Failure to comply with a special requirement as to the displaying of lights imposed by a transport authority under s. 92(1)	level 5

Provision specifying fine	*Brief description of offence or offences to which the fine relates*	*New maximum fine*
Schedule 3, paragraph 5(3)	Failure to comply with obligation under paragraph 5 (obligations to give notice to street authority)	level 4
Schedule 4, paragraph 6	Execution of works in street with special engineering difficulties in contravention of paragraph 2 (requirement for agreed plan and section before executing works) or paragraph 3 (requirement to furnish plan and section after emergency works)	level 5
Schedule 4, paragraph 12(5)	Failure to execute works in such a street in accordance with a direction under paragraph 12	level 5
Schedule 4, paragraph 13(2)	Failure to comply with paragraph 13(1) (requirement to execute works in such a street in accordance with plan or agreed modification)	level 5

SCHEDULE 2

Section 41

SCHEDULE 4A TO THE NEW ROADS AND STREET WORKS ACT 1991

"SCHEDULE 4A

Section 95A

FIXED PENALTY OFFENCES UNDER PART 3

Offence	*Brief description*
An offence under section 54(5)	Failure to comply with duties under s. 54 (advance notice of certain works, etc.)
An offence under section 55(5)	Beginning to execute works in contravention of s. 55 (notice of starting date)
An offence under section 55(9)	Failure to give notice in accordance with s. 55(8) (notice to be given on s. 55 notice ceasing to have effect)
An offence under section 57(4)	Failure to give notice in accordance with s. 57 (notice of emergency works)

Offence	*Brief description*
An offence under section 70(6) consisting of a failure to comply with subsection (3) or (4A)	Failure to comply with requirements to give notice of completion of reinstatement
An offence created by regulations made under section 74(7B)	Failure to give a notice required by regulations under s. 74 (charge for occupation of the highway where works unreasonably delayed)
An offence created by regulations made under section 74A(11)	Failure to give a notice required by regulations under s. 74A (charge determined by reference to duration of works)"

SCHEDULE 3

Section 41

SCHEDULE 4B TO THE NEW ROADS AND STREET WORKS ACT 1991

"SCHEDULE 4B

Section 95A

FIXED PENALTIES FOR CERTAIN OFFENCES UNDER PART 3

1 Power to give fixed penalty notices

1 (1) An authorised officer of a street authority may, if he has reason to believe that a person is committing or has committed a fixed penalty offence, give him a fixed penalty notice in relation to that offence.

(2) In this Schedule "fixed penalty notice" means a notice offering a person the opportunity of discharging any liability to conviction for a fixed penalty offence by payment of a penalty.

2 A fixed penalty notice for an offence may not be given after such time relating to the offence as the Secretary of State may by regulations prescribe.

3 Contents of fixed penalty notice

3 (1) A fixed penalty notice must identify the offence to which it relates and give reasonable particulars of the circumstances alleged to constitute that offence.

(2) A fixed penalty notice must also state—

(a) the amount of the penalty and the period within which it may be paid;

(b) the discounted amount and the period within which it may be paid;

(c) the person to whom and the address at which payment may be made;

(d) the method or methods by which payment may be made;

(e) the person to whom and the address at which any representations relating to the notice may be addressed;

(f) the consequences of not making a payment within the period for payment.

(3) The person specified under sub-paragraph (2)(c) must be the street authority or a person acting on their behalf.

4 The amount of the penalty and the period for payment

4 (1) The penalty for a fixed penalty offence is (subject to paragraph 5) such amount, not exceeding 30 per cent. of the maximum fine for that offence, as may be prescribed.

(2) The period for payment of the penalty is the period of 29 days beginning with the day on which the notice is given.

(3) The street authority may extend the period for paying the penalty in any particular case if they consider it appropriate to do so.

5 The discounted amount

5 (1) A discounted amount is payable instead of the amount prescribed under paragraph 4(1) if payment is made before the end of the period of 15 days beginning with the day on which the notice is given.

(2) The discounted amount for a fixed penalty offence is such amount, not exceeding 25 per cent. of the maximum fine for the offence, as may be prescribed.

(3) If the last day of the period specified in sub-paragraph (1) does not fall on a working day, the period for payment of the discounted amount is extended until the end of the next working day.

6 Effect of notice and payment of penalty

6 (1) This paragraph applies where a person is given a fixed penalty notice in respect of a fixed penalty offence.

(2) No proceedings for the offence may be commenced before the end of the period for payment of the penalty.

(3) No such proceedings may be commenced or continued if payment of the penalty is made before the end of that period or is accepted by the street authority after that time.

(4) Payment of the discounted amount only counts for the purposes of sub-paragraph (3) if it is made before the end of the period for payment of the discounted amount.

(5) In proceedings for the offence a certificate which—

(a) purports to be signed by or on behalf of the person having responsibility for the financial affairs of the street authority; and

(b) states that payment of an amount specified in the certificate was or was not received by a date so specified,

is evidence of the facts stated.

7 Power to withdraw notices

7 (1) If the street authority consider that a fixed penalty notice which has been given ought not to have been given, they may give to the person to whom it was given a notice withdrawing the fixed penalty notice.

(2) Where a notice under sub-paragraph (1) is given—

(a) the authority shall repay any amount which has been paid by way of penalty in pursuance of the fixed penalty notice; and

(b) no proceedings shall be commenced or continued against that person for the offence in question.

(3) The street authority shall consider any representations made by or on behalf of the recipient of a fixed penalty notice and decide in all the circumstances whether to withdraw the notice.

8 General and supplementary

8 The Secretary of State may, with the consent of the Treasury, make regulations about—

(a) the application by street authorities of fixed penalties paid under this Schedule;

(b) the keeping of accounts, and the preparation and publication of statements of account, relating to fixed penalties paid under this Schedule.

9 The Secretary of State may by regulations—

(a) prescribe circumstances in which fixed penalty notices may not be given;

(b) modify paragraph 4(2) or 5(1) so as to substitute a different period for the period for the time being specified there;

(c) prescribe the method or methods by which penalties may be paid."

SCHEDULE 4

Section 52

SCHEDULE 3A TO THE NEW ROADS AND STREET WORKS ACT 1991

"SCHEDULE 3A

RESTRICTION ON WORKS FOLLOWING SUBSTANTIAL STREET WORKS

1 Introductory

1 (1) This Schedule applies where a street authority receive a notice under section 54 or 55 that an undertaker is proposing to execute substantial street works in a highway.

(2) For the purposes of this Schedule, "substantial street works" means street works of such description as may be prescribed.

2 Notice by authority of proposed restriction

2 (1) The street authority may publish a notice—

(a) specifying the nature and location of the proposed works and the date on which it is proposed to begin them;

(b) stating that the authority propose to issue a direction under paragraph 4 imposing a restriction on street works;

(c) stating the duration of the proposed restriction and the part of the highway to which it relates;

(d) requiring any other undertakers who propose to execute street works in that part of the highway, and who have not already done so, to notify the authority of their proposed works within the period specified in the notice ("the notice period").

(2) The notice period shall not be less than such period as may be prescribed.

(3) A notice under this paragraph shall—

(a) be published in the prescribed form and manner; and

(b) comply with such requirements as to its form and content as may be prescribed.

(4) A copy of a notice under this paragraph shall be given to each of the following—

(a) where there is a public sewer in the part of the highway specified under sub-paragraph (1)(c), to the sewer authority;

(b) where that part of the highway is carried or crossed by a bridge vested in a transport authority, or crosses or is crossed by any other property held by or used for the purposes of a transport authority, to that authority;

(c) where in any other case that part of the highway is carried or crossed by a bridge, to the bridge authority;

(d) any person who has given notice under section 54 of his intention to execute street works in that part of the highway;

(e) any person who has apparatus in that part of the highway;

(f) any other person of a prescribed description.

(5) Notification under sub-paragraph (1)(d) shall be in such form, contain such information, and be made in such manner as may be prescribed.

(6) Section 55 does not apply in relation to works in the part of the highway specified under sub-paragraph (1)(c) that are begun between the end of the notice period and completion of the works referred to in paragraph 3(1)(a) to (c).

This sub-paragraph does not apply to cases prescribed under paragraph 3(5)(b).

3 Completion of notified works

3 (1) After the expiry of the notice period the street authority may issue directions to—

(a) the undertaker proposing to execute the substantial street works,

(b) any undertakers who have given notice under paragraph 2 in respect of works they propose to execute, and

(c) any undertakers who have previously given notice of works they propose to execute in the part of the highway specified under paragraph 2(1)(c).

(2) A direction to an undertaker under this paragraph is a direction as to the date on which he may begin to execute the works proposed by him.

(3) Where—

(a) a direction is given to an undertaker under this paragraph as respects the date on which he may begin to execute the works proposed by him, and

(b) he begins to execute those works before that date,

he is guilty of an offence.

(4) After the expiry of the notice period, any undertaker who, before completion of the works referred to in sub-paragraph (1)(a) to (c), executes any other street works in the part of the highway specified under paragraph 2(1)(c), commits an offence.

(5) Sub-paragraph (4) does not apply—
(a) where an undertaker executes emergency works; or
(b) in such other cases as may be prescribed.

(6) A person guilty of an offence under this paragraph is liable on summary conviction to a fine not exceeding level 5 on the standard scale.

4 Direction restricting further works

4 (1) After the expiry of the notice period and before completion of the works referred to in paragraph 3(1)(a) to (c) the authority may give a direction under this paragraph.

(2) A direction under this paragraph is a direction restricting the execution of street works in the part of the highway specified under paragraph 2(1)(c) for such period following completion of the works referred to in paragraph 3(1)(a) to (c) as may be specified in the direction.

(3) The duration of the period specified under sub-paragraph (2) may not exceed the duration of the restriction proposed by the authority under paragraph 2(1)(c).

(4) The period specified in a direction under this paragraph may not in any case exceed such period as may be prescribed.

(5) A direction under this paragraph shall—
(a) be given in the prescribed manner;
(b) comply with such requirements as to its form and content as may be prescribed.

(6) The street authority must send a copy of any direction under this paragraph to the persons specified in paragraph 2(4).

(7) A direction under this paragraph shall cease to have effect if the works referred to in paragraph 3(1)(a) to (c) to which it relates are not completed within such period as may be prescribed.

(8) A direction under this paragraph may be revoked at any time by the authority which gave it.

(9) Where a direction under this paragraph ceases to have effect by virtue of sub-paragraph (7), or is revoked by virtue of sub-paragraph (8), the street authority must notify the persons specified in paragraph 2(4).

(10) If the street authority decides not to give a direction under this paragraph, it must notify the persons specified in paragraph 2(4) accordingly.

5 Effect of direction imposing restriction

5 (1) Where a direction under paragraph 4 is in force, an undertaker may not during the period specified in the direction execute street works in the part of the highway to which the restriction relates.

(2) Sub-paragraph (1) does not apply—
(a) where an undertaker executes emergency works;
(b) where an undertaker executes works with the consent of the street authority; or

(c) in such other cases as may be prescribed.

(3) The consent of the street authority under sub-paragraph (2)(b) shall not be unreasonably withheld; and any question whether the withholding of consent is unreasonable shall be settled in such manner as may be prescribed.

(4) Regulations under sub-paragraph (3) may in particular make provision for the question referred to in that sub-paragraph to be settled—

(a) by arbitration;

(b) by a person specified by the Secretary of State on appeal by the undertaker.

(5) An undertaker who contravenes sub-paragraph (1) commits an offence and is liable on summary conviction to a fine not exceeding level 5 on the standard scale.

(6) An undertaker convicted of an offence under sub-paragraph (5) is liable to reimburse the street authority any costs reasonably incurred by them in reinstating the highway.

6 Supplementary

6 An undertaker shall be taken not to have failed to fulfil any statutory duty to afford a supply or service if, or to the extent that, his failure is attributable to a restriction imposed under this Schedule."

SCHEDULE 5

Section 64

SCHEDULE 22A TO THE HIGHWAYS ACT 1980

"SCHEDULE 22A

Section 314A

FIXED PENALTY OFFENCES UNDER PART 9

Offence	*Brief description*
An offence under section 139(3)	Deposit of builder's skip on highway without permission of highway authority.
An offence under section 139(4)	Failure of owner of skip to ensure skip properly lit and marked and removed as soon as practicable once filled or to ensure conditions of permission complied with.
An offence created by regulations made under section 140A, consisting of a failure to give a notice	Failure to give a notice required by regulations under s.140A (charge for occupation of the highway by builder's skip for unreasonable period).
An offence created by regulations made under section 140B, consisting of a failure to give a notice	Failure to give a notice required by regulations under s.140B (charge determined by reference to duration of occupation of the highway by builder's skip).

Offence	*Brief description*
An offence under section 169(5)	Offences relating to the erection or retention of scaffolding etc. which obstructs the highway.
An offence under section 170(1)	Mixing or depositing mortar etc. on highway.
An offence under section 171(6)	Offences relating to the deposit of materials on highway or the making of temporary excavations in it.
An offence created by regulations made under section 171A, consisting of a failure to give a notice	Failure to give a notice required by regulations under s.171A (charge for occupation of the highway by scaffolding etc. for unreasonable period).
An offence created by regulations made under section 171B, consisting of a failure to give a notice	Failure to give a notice required by regulations under s.171B (charge determined by reference to duration of occupation of the highway by scaffolding etc.)."

SCHEDULE 6

Section 64

SCHEDULE 22B TO THE HIGHWAYS ACT 1980

"SCHEDULE 22B

Section 314A

FIXED PENALTIES FOR CERTAIN OFFENCES UNDER PART 9

1 Power to give fixed penalty notices

1 (1) An authorised officer of a highway authority may, if he has reason to believe that a person is committing or has committed a fixed penalty offence, give him a fixed penalty notice in relation to that offence.

(2) In this Schedule "fixed penalty notice" means a notice offering a person the opportunity of discharging any liability to conviction for a fixed penalty offence by payment of a penalty.

2 A fixed penalty notice for an offence may not be given after such time relating to the offence as the Secretary of State may by regulations prescribe.

3 Contents of fixed penalty notice

3 (1) A fixed penalty notice must identify the offence to which it relates and give reasonable particulars of the circumstances alleged to constitute that offence.

(2) A fixed penalty notice must also state—

(a) the amount of the penalty and the period within which it may be paid;

(b) the discounted amount and the period within which it may be paid;

(c) the person to whom and the address at which payment may be made;

(d) the method or methods by which payment may be made;

(e) the person to whom and the address at which any representations relating to the notice may be addressed;

(f) the consequences of not making any payment within the period for payment.

(3) The person specified under sub-paragraph (2)(c) must be the highway authority or a person acting on their behalf.

4 The amount of the penalty and the period for payment

4 (1) The penalty for a fixed penalty offence is (subject to paragraph 5) such amount, not exceeding 30 per cent. of the maximum fine for that offence, as may be prescribed.

(2) The period for payment of the penalty is the period of 29 days beginning with the day on which the notice is given.

(3) The highway authority may extend the period for paying the penalty in any particular case if they consider it appropriate to do so.

5 The discounted amount

5 (1) A discounted amount is payable instead of the amount prescribed under paragraph 4(1) if payment is made before the end of the period of 15 days beginning with the day on which the notice is given.

(2) The discounted amount for a fixed penalty offence is such amount, not exceeding 25 per cent. of the maximum fine for the offence, as may be prescribed.

(3) If the last day of the period specified in sub-paragraph (1) does not fall on a working day, the period for payment of the discounted amount is extended until the end of the next working day.

(4) In sub-paragraph (3) "working day" means a day other than a Saturday, a Sunday, Christmas Day, Good Friday or a bank holiday in the locality in which the highway in question is situated.

6 Effect of notice and payment of penalty

6 (1) This paragraph applies where a person is given a fixed penalty notice in respect of a fixed penalty offence.

(2) No proceedings for the offence may be commenced before the end of the period for payment of the penalty.

(3) No such proceedings may be commenced or continued if payment of the penalty is made before the end of that period or is accepted by the highway authority after that time.

(4) Payment of the discounted amount only counts for the purposes of sub-paragraph (3) if it is made before the end of the period for payment of the discounted amount.

(5) In proceedings for the offence a certificate which—

(a) purports to be signed by or on behalf of the person having responsibility for the financial affairs of the highway authority; and

(b) states that payment of an amount specified in the certificate was or was not received by a date so specified,

is evidence of the facts stated.

7 Power to withdraw notices

7 (1) If the highway authority consider that a fixed penalty notice which has been given ought not to have been given, they may give to the person on whom it was given a notice withdrawing the fixed penalty notice.

(2) Where a notice under sub-paragraph (1) is given—

(a) the authority shall repay any amount which has been paid by way of penalty in pursuance of the fixed penalty notice; and

(b) no proceedings may be commenced or continued against that person for the offence in question.

(3) The highway authority shall consider any representations made by or on behalf of the recipient of a fixed penalty notice and decide in all the circumstances whether to withdraw the notice.

8 General and supplementary

8 (1) In this Schedule "prescribed" means prescribed in regulations made by the Secretary of State.

(2) The Secretary of State may, with the consent of the Treasury, make regulations about—

(a) the application by highway authorities of fixed penalties paid under this Schedule;

(b) the keeping of accounts, and the preparation and publication of statements of account, relating to penalties paid under this Schedule.

(3) The Secretary of State may by regulations—

(a) prescribe circumstances in which fixed penalty notices may not be given;

(b) modify paragraph 4(2) or 5(1) so as to substitute a different period for the period for the time being specified there;

(c) prescribe the method or methods by which penalties may be paid.

(4) Regulations under this Schedule may—

(a) make different provision (including provision prescribing the amount of the penalty or the discounted amount) for different purposes or areas;

(b) make consequential or transitional provision.

9 Section 323(1)(b) (reckoning of periods of 8 days or less) does not apply for the purposes of this Schedule."

Status: This is the original version (as it was originally enacted).

SCHEDULE 7

Section 73

ROAD TRAFFIC CONTRAVENTIONS SUBJECT TO CIVIL ENFORCEMENT

PART 1

PARKING CONTRAVENTIONS

Parking contraventions

1 References in this Part of this Act to a parking contravention shall be construed as follows.

Contraventions relating to parking places in Greater London

2 (1) In Greater London there is a parking contravention in relation to a vehicle if the vehicle is stationary in a parking place and—

(a) the vehicle has been left—

(i) otherwise than as authorised by or under any order relating to the parking place, or

(ii) beyond the period of parking that has been paid for,

(b) no parking charge payable with respect to the vehicle has been paid, or

(c) there has been, with respect to the vehicle, a contravention of any provision made by or under any order relating to the parking place.

(2) In sub-paragraph (1) "parking place" means—

(a) a parking place designated by an order made under section 6, 9 or 45 of the Road Traffic Regulation Act 1984 (c. 27), or

(b) an off-street parking place provided under section 32(1)(a) of that Act.

Other parking contraventions in Greater London

3 (1) In Greater London there is a parking contravention in relation to a vehicle if it is stationary in circumstances in which any of the offences listed below is committed.

(2) The offences are—

(a) an offence under section 15 of the Greater London Council (General Powers) Act 1974 (c. xxiv) (parking on footways, verges, etc.);

(b) an offence under section 8, 11, 16(1) or 16C of the Road Traffic Regulation Act 1984 (contravention of certain traffic orders) of contravening—

(i) a prohibition or restriction on waiting of vehicles, or

(ii) provision relating to any of the matters mentioned in paragraph 7 or 8 of Schedule 1 to that Act (conditions for loading or unloading, or delivering or collecting);

(c) an offence under section 25(5) of the Road Traffic Regulation Act 1984 of contravening regulation 18 or 20 of the Zebra, Pelican and Puffin Pedestrian Crossings Regulations and General Directions 1997 (S.I. 1997/2400) (prohibition on stopping vehicles on or near pedestrian crossings);

(d) an offence under section 35A(1) of the Road Traffic Regulation Act 1984 (contravention of orders relating to parking places provided under section 32 or 33 of that Act);
(e) an offence under section 61(5) of the Road Traffic Regulation Act 1984 (parking in loading areas);
(f) an offence under section 19 of the Road Traffic Act 1988 (c. 52) (parking of HGVs on verges, central reservations or footways);
(g) an offence under section 21 of the Road Traffic Act 1988 (offences relating to cycle tracks) of parking a vehicle wholly or partly on a cycle track;
(h) an offence under section 36(1) of the Road Traffic Act 1988 (failure to comply with traffic sign) of failing to comply with a sign of a type referred to in—
(i) regulation 10(1)(b) of the Traffic Signs Regulations and General Directions 2002 (S.I. 2002/3113) (zig-zag lines relating to certain crossings), or
(ii) regulation 29(1) of those regulations (bus stop or bus stand markings).

(3) This paragraph does not apply to a contravention within paragraph 2 above (contraventions relating to parking places).

Parking contraventions outside Greater London

4 (1) Outside Greater London there is a parking contravention in relation to a vehicle if it is stationary in circumstances in which any of the offences listed below is committed.

(2) The offences are—
(a) an offence under section 64(3) of the Local Government (Miscellaneous Provisions) Act 1976 (c. 57) of causing a vehicle to stop on part of a road appointed, or deemed to have been appointed, as a hackney carriage stand;
(b) an offence under section 5, 11, 16(1) or 16C of the Road Traffic Regulation Act 1984 (c. 27) (contravention of certain traffic orders) of contravening a prohibition or restriction on waiting, or loading or unloading, of vehicles;
(c) an offence under section 25(5) of the Road Traffic Regulation Act 1984 of contravening regulation 18 or 20 of the Zebra, Pelican and Puffin Pedestrian Crossings Regulations and General Directions 1997 (S.I. 1997/2400) (prohibition on stopping vehicles on or near pedestrian crossings);
(d) an offence under section 35A(1), 47(1) or 53(5) or (6) of the Road Traffic Regulation Act 1984 (offences in connection with parking places);
(e) an offence under section 61(5) of the Road Traffic Regulation Act 1984 (parking in loading areas);
(f) an offence under section 6(6) of the Essex Act 1987 (c. xx) of leaving a vehicle on any land in contravention of a prohibition under that section (prohibitions relating to verges and certain other land adjoining or accessible from highway);
(g) an offence under section 19 of the Road Traffic Act 1988 (c. 52) (parking of HGVs on verges, central reservations or footways);
(h) an offence under section 21 of the Road Traffic Act 1988 (offences relating to cycle tracks) of parking a vehicle wholly or partly on a cycle track;

(i) an offence under section 36(1) of the Road Traffic Act 1988 (failure to comply with traffic sign) of failing to comply with a sign of a type referred to in—

(i) regulation 10(1)(b) of the Traffic Signs Regulations and General Directions 2002 (S.I. 2002/3113) (zig-zag lines relating to certain crossings), or

(ii) regulation 29(1) of those regulations (bus stop or bus stand markings).

Power to add further offences

5 (1) The appropriate national authority may by regulations amend paragraph 3 or 4 so as to add further offences (but only in so far as they relate to stationary vehicles).

(2) Before making regulations amending paragraph 3 the Secretary of State shall consult—

(a) the Commissioner of Police of the Metropolis and the Commissioner of Police for the City of London, and

(b) such associations of London authorities (if any) as he thinks appropriate.

(3) Before making regulations amending paragraph 4 the appropriate national authority shall consult—

(a) such representatives of chief officers of police, and

(b) such associations of local authorities (if any),

as the authority considers appropriate.

PART 2

BUS LANE CONTRAVENTIONS

Bus lane contraventions

6 (1) A bus lane contravention is a contravention of any provision of a traffic order relating to the use of an area of road that is or forms part of a bus lane.

(2) An area of road is or forms part of a bus lane if the order provides that it may be used—

(a) only by buses (or a particular description of bus), or

(b) only by buses (or a particular description of bus) and some other class or classes of vehicular traffic.

(3) In this paragraph—

"bus" includes a tramcar (within the meaning of section 141A of the Road Traffic Regulation Act 1984 (c. 27)) and a trolley vehicle (within the meaning of that section); and

"traffic order" means an order under section 1, 6, 9 or 14 of that Act.

PART 3

LONDON LORRY BAN CONTRAVENTIONS

London lorry ban contraventions

7 A London lorry ban contravention is a contravention of the Greater London (Restriction of Goods Vehicles) Traffic Order 1985 made by the Greater London Council under section 6 of the Road Traffic Regulation Act 1984, or any order replacing that order, as amended from time to time.

PART 4

MOVING TRAFFIC CONTRAVENTIONS

Moving traffic contraventions

8 (1) A moving traffic contravention is—

(a) an offence under section 36 of the Road Traffic Act 1988 (c. 52) of failing to comply with the indication given by a traffic sign that is subject to civil enforcement (see paragraph 9), or

(b) an offence of failing to comply with a traffic order in so far as it makes provision for a requirement, restriction or prohibition that is conveyed by a traffic sign subject to civil enforcement.

(2) In sub-paragraph (1)(b) "traffic order" means an order under section 1, 6, 9, 14 or 16A of the Road Traffic Regulation Act 1984 (c. 27).

(3) If conduct is both a moving traffic contravention and a London lorry ban contravention (see Part 3 above), a penalty charge may only be imposed on the latter basis.

(4) If in any other case the same conduct is a moving traffic contravention under sub-paragraph (1)(a) and (b), a penalty charge may be imposed on either basis but not both.

Traffic signs subject to civil enforcement

9 (1) The table below specifies the traffic signs that are subject to civil enforcement.

(2) In the table—

(a) column 1 sets out the description, corresponding to the description in the Traffic Signs Regulations and General Directions 2002 (S.I. 2002/3113), of the requirement, restriction or prohibition conveyed by the sign, and

(b) column 2 sets out the number given to the diagram illustrating the sign in that instrument.

(3) References in the table to any sign include any permitted variant of that sign.

(4) The table is as follows:

Description	*Diagram number*
Vehicular traffic must proceed in the direction indicated by the arrow	606
Vehicular traffic must turn ahead in the direction indicated by the arrow	609
Vehicular traffic must comply with the requirements in regulation 15	610
No right turn for vehicular traffic	612
No left turn for vehicular traffic	613
No U-turns for vehicular traffic	614
Priority must be given to vehicles from the opposite direction	615, 615.1
No entry for vehicular traffic (when the restriction or prohibition is one that may be indicated by another traffic sign subject to civil enforcement)	616
All vehicles prohibited except non-mechanically propelled vehicles being pushed by pedestrians	617
Entry to pedestrian zone restricted (alternative types)	618.2
Entry to and waiting in pedestrian zone restricted (alternative types)	618.3
Entry to and waiting in pedestrian zone restricted (variable message sign)	618.3A
Motor vehicles prohibited	619
Motor vehicles except solo motor cycles prohibited	619.1
Solo motor cycles prohibited	619.2
Goods vehicles exceeding the maximum gross weight indicated on the goods vehicle symbol prohibited	622.1A
One way traffic	652
Buses prohibited	952
Route for use by buses and pedal cycles only	953
Route for use by tramcars only	953.1
Route for use by pedal cycles only	955
Route for use by pedal cycles and pedestrians only	956

Description	*Diagram number*
Route comprising two ways, for use by pedal cycles only and by pedestrians only	957
With-flow cycle lane	959.1
Contra-flow cycle lane	960.1
Box junction markings	1043, 1044

Power to amend table

10 (1) The appropriate national authority may by regulations amend the table in paragraph 9(4) so as to add further traffic signs.

(2) A traffic sign may only be added to the table if it is of a type—

(a) regulating the movement of vehicles (and not stationary vehicles),

(b) to which section 36 of the Road Traffic Act 1988 (c. 52) applies (offence of failure to comply with traffic sign), and

(c) failure to comply with which is not an offence involving obligatory endorsement.

In paragraph (c) "offence involving obligatory endorsement" has the meaning given by section 96 of the Road Traffic Offenders Act 1988 (c. 53).

(3) Before making regulations under this paragraph the appropriate national authority shall consult—

(a) such representatives of chief officers of police, and

(b) such associations of local authorities (if any),

as the authority considers appropriate.

SCHEDULE 8

Section 74

CIVIL ENFORCEMENT AREAS AND ENFORCEMENT AUTHORITIES

PART 1

IN GREATER LONDON

Civil enforcement of parking contraventions relating to parking places

1 (1) The whole of Greater London is a civil enforcement area for parking contraventions within paragraph 2 of Schedule 7 (contraventions relating to parking places).

(2) References in this Part of this Act to the enforcement authority in relation to such contraventions are to the authority by whom the parking place in question was designated or provided.

Civil enforcement of other parking contraventions

2 (1) The Secretary of State may, on an application by a London authority, make an order designating the whole or part of the authority's area as a civil enforcement area for parking contraventions within paragraph 3 of Schedule 7 (contraventions other than those relating to parking places).

(2) An application may be made—

(a) by Transport for London, to the extent that the civil enforcement area is to consist of GLA roads;

(b) by a London local authority, to the extent that the civil enforcement area is to consist of roads other than GLA roads.

(3) Before making an order under this paragraph the Secretary of State shall consult the Commissioner of Police of the Metropolis or the Commissioner of Police for the City of London or, if appropriate, both of them.

(4) An order in force immediately before the commencement of this Part of this Act designating an area in Greater London as a special parking area under section 76 of the Road Traffic Act 1991 (c. 40) has effect on and after the commencement of this Part of this Act as if it were an order under this paragraph designating that area as a civil enforcement area for such parking contraventions as are mentioned in sub-paragraph (1).

(5) References in this Part of this Act to the enforcement authority in relation to such contraventions in Greater London are—

(a) as respects parking, or any matter connected with or relating to parking, on or adjacent to a GLA road, to Transport for London;

(b) as respects parking, or any matter connected with or relating to parking, on or adjacent to a road other than a GLA road, to the London local authority in whose area the road is situated.

Variation of civil enforcement area by Mayor of London

3 (1) The Mayor of London may by order under this paragraph amend an order for the time being in force under paragraph 2 so as to vary the area that for the time being constitutes the civil enforcement area.

(2) No such order may be made without the consent of the relevant London authority for every road that the order has the effect of bringing within, or removing from, the civil enforcement area.

(3) The relevant London authority is—

(a) as regards GLA roads, Transport for London;

(b) as regards roads other than GLA roads, the London local authority in whose area the road is situated.

(4) An order under this paragraph must not be such as to bring within a civil enforcement area an area as to which the Secretary of State has specified by order that it is expedient on grounds of national security that no part of it should be included in a civil enforcement area.

(5) An order in force immediately before the commencement of this Part of this Act under section 76A(1) or (3)(a) of the Road Traffic Act 1991 (c. 40) has effect on and

after the commencement of this Part of this Act as if made under the corresponding provision of this paragraph.

Civil enforcement of bus lane contraventions

4 (1) The whole of Greater London is a civil enforcement area for bus lane contraventions.

(2) References in this Part of this Act to the enforcement authority in relation to bus lane contraventions in Greater London are—

(a) in relation to contraventions on GLA roads, to Transport for London or the relevant London local authority acting with the written consent of Transport for London;

(b) in relation to contraventions on roads other than GLA roads, to the relevant London local authority or Transport for London acting with the written consent of the relevant London local authority.

(3) Consent under sub-paragraph (2)(a) or (b) may be given with respect to the whole or part of the area of the relevant London local authority.

(4) In this paragraph "the relevant London local authority" means the London local authority in whose area the contravention is committed.

(5) Any consent in force immediately before the commencement of this Part of this Act for the purposes of the provisions of regulations under section 144 of the Transport Act 2000 (c. 38) corresponding to the provisions of this paragraph has effect on and after the commencement of this Part of this Act as if given under this paragraph.

Civil enforcement of London lorry ban contraventions

5 (1) The whole of Greater London is a civil enforcement area for London lorry ban contraventions.

(2) References in this Part of this Act to the enforcement authority in relation to such contraventions are—

(a) in relation to contraventions on GLA roads, to Transport for London;

(b) in relation to contraventions on roads other than GLA roads, to the London local authority in whose area the contravention is committed.

Civil enforcement of moving traffic contraventions: London local authorities

6 (1) A London local authority may by resolution declare the whole or part of its area to be a civil enforcement area for moving traffic contraventions.

(2) The resolution must specify the date on which it is to have effect, which must be not less than three months after publication of the notice required by sub-paragraph (3).

(3) The authority shall cause notice to be published in a local newspaper circulating in their area—

(a) of the passing of the resolution, and

(b) of the general effect of the provisions of this Act coming into operation as a result of it.

(4) A photocopy or other reproduction certified by the officer appointed for that purpose by the authority to be a reproduction of a page or part of a page of any such newspaper

bearing the date of its publication and containing any such notice shall be evidence of the publication of the notice and of the date of publication.

(5) A civil enforcement area declared by resolution under this paragraph does not extend to any GLA road.

(6) In relation to moving traffic contraventions in a civil enforcement area created by resolution under this paragraph, references in this Part of this Act to the enforcement authority are to the London local authority by whom the resolution was passed or Transport for London acting with the written consent of that authority.

Consent may be given with respect to the whole or part of the area of the London local authority.

Civil enforcement of moving traffic contraventions: Transport for London

7 (1) Transport for London may declare the whole or part of one or more GLA roads to be a civil enforcement area for moving traffic contraventions.

(2) The declaration must specify the date on which it is to have effect, which must be not less than three months after publication of the notice required by sub-paragraph (3).

(3) Transport for London shall cause notice to be published in a local newspaper circulating in the area of each London local authority in which a road, or part of a road, to which the declaration relates is situated—

(a) of the making of the declaration, and

(b) of the general effect of the provisions of this Act coming into operation as a result of it.

(4) A photocopy or other reproduction certified by the officer appointed for that purpose by Transport for London to be a reproduction of a page or part of a page of any such newspaper bearing the date of its publication and containing any such notice shall be evidence of the publication of the notice and of the date of publication.

(5) In relation to moving traffic contraventions in a civil enforcement area declared under this paragraph, references in this Part of this Act to the enforcement authority are to Transport for London or the London local authority in whose area the contravention is committed acting with the written consent of Transport for London.

Consent may be given with respect to the whole or part of the area of a London local authority.

PART 2

OUTSIDE GREATER LONDON

Designation of civil enforcement areas for parking contraventions

8 (1) The appropriate national authority may, on an application under this paragraph, make an order designating the whole or part of a local authority's area as a civil enforcement area for parking contraventions.

(2) An application under this paragraph may be made—

(a) with respect to the whole or part of their area, by a county council in England;

(b) with respect to the whole or part of their area, by a county council or county borough council in Wales;

(c) with respect to the whole of their area, by a metropolitan district council;

(d) with respect to the whole of their areas, by two or more metropolitan district councils acting jointly;

(e) with respect to the whole or part of the Isles of Scilly, by the Council of the Isles of Scilly.

(3) Before making an order under this paragraph the appropriate national authority shall consult the appropriate chief officer of police.

(4) An order in force immediately before the commencement of this Part of this Act designating an area outside Greater London as a permitted parking area and special parking area under paragraphs 1(1) and 2(1) of Schedule 3 to the Road Traffic Act 1991 (c. 40) has effect on and after the commencement of this Part of this Act as an order under this paragraph designating the area as a civil enforcement area for parking contraventions.

(5) References in this Part of this Act to the enforcement authority in relation to parking contraventions in a civil enforcement area outside Greater London, are—

(a) in relation to contraventions relating to a parking place—

(i) provided or authorised under section 32(1)(a) or (b) of the Road Traffic Regulation Act 1984 (c. 27), or

(ii) designated by order under section 45 of that Act,

to the authority by whom the parking place was provided, authorised or designated;

(b) in relation to other parking contraventions, to the local authority in whose area the contravention is committed.

Designation of civil enforcement areas for bus lane contraventions

9 (1) The appropriate national authority may make an order designating the whole or part of a local authority's area as a civil enforcement area for bus lane contraventions.

(2) An area may only be so designated if it is within, or is co-extensive with, an area already designated as a civil enforcement area for parking contraventions.

(3) An order in force immediately before the commencement of this Part of this Act approving a local authority for the purposes of section 144 of the Transport Act 2000 (c. 38) (civil penalties for bus lane contraventions) has effect on and after the commencement of this Part of this Act as an order under this paragraph designating as a civil enforcement area for bus lane contraventions so much of that authority's area as is a civil enforcement area for parking contraventions.

(4) References in this Part of this Act to the enforcement authority in relation to bus lane contraventions outside Greater London are to the local authority in whose area the contravention is committed.

Designation of civil enforcement areas for moving traffic contraventions

10 (1) The appropriate national authority may, on an application under this paragraph, make an order designating the whole or part of a local authority's area as a civil enforcement area for moving traffic contraventions.

(2) An area may only be so designated if it is within, or is co-extensive with, an area already designated as a civil enforcement area for parking contraventions.

(3) An application under this paragraph may be made—

(a) with respect to the whole or part of their area, by a county council in England;

(b) with respect to the whole or part of their area, by a county council or county borough council in Wales;

(c) with respect to the whole or part of their area, by a metropolitan district council;

(d) with respect to the whole of their areas, by two or more metropolitan district councils acting jointly;

(e) with respect to the whole or part of the Isles of Scilly, by the Council of the Isles of Scilly.

(4) Before making an order under this paragraph the appropriate national authority shall consult the appropriate chief officer of police.

(5) In relation to a civil enforcement area designated by order under this paragraph, references in this Part of this Act to the enforcement authority are to the authority on whose application the order was made or, if the application was a joint application, any of the authorities on whose application the order was made.

SCHEDULE 9

Section 77

CIVIL ENFORCEMENT: SETTING THE LEVEL OF CHARGES

PART 1

CHARGES TO WHICH THIS SCHEDULE APPLIES

Charges to which this Schedule applies

1 (1) This Schedule provides for the setting of the levels of—

(a) penalty charges, including any discounts or surcharges,

(b) charges made by authorities under section 102 of the Road Traffic Regulation Act 1984 (c. 27) for the removal, storage and disposal of vehicles found in areas that are civil enforcement areas for parking contraventions, and

(c) charges for the release of vehicles from an immobilisation device under regulations under section 79 above.

(2) References in this Schedule to "charges" are to those charges.

PART 2

CHARGES APPLICABLE IN GREATER LONDON

Charges to be set by Transport for London or London local authorities

2 (1) It is the duty—

(a) of Transport for London, so far as relating to contraventions on or adjacent to GLA roads, and

(b) of the London local authorities, so far as relating to—

(i) parking places provided or authorised by such authorities, or

(ii) contraventions on or adjacent to roads other than GLA roads,

to set the levels of charges applicable in Greater London.

(2) Different levels of charges may be set for different areas in London and for different cases or classes of case.

(3) Before setting the level of any charges Transport for London must consult the London local authorities.

Supervisory role of Mayor of London

3 (1) Transport for London and the London local authorities must submit to the Mayor of London for his approval the levels of charges that they propose to set.

(2) If—

(a) Transport for London or the London local authorities fail to discharge their duty under paragraph 2, or

(b) the Mayor of London does not approve the levels of charges proposed by the London local authorities,

the levels of charges shall be set by order made by the Mayor of London.

Reserve powers of Secretary of State

4 (1) The following provisions apply where the Mayor of London—

(a) approves any levels of charges on a submission under paragraph 3(1), or

(b) sets any such levels under paragraph 3(2).

(2) The Mayor must notify the Secretary of State of the levels of charges so approved or set.

(3) The levels of charges shall not come into force until after the expiration of—

(a) the period of one month beginning with the date on which the notification is given, or

(b) such shorter period as the Secretary of State may allow.

(4) The Secretary of State may before the end of that period give notice to the Mayor of London that he objects to the levels of charges on the grounds that some or all of them are excessive.

If he does so those levels of charges shall not come into force unless and until the objection has been withdrawn.

(5) If at any time before the levels of charges have come into force, the Secretary of State considers that some or all of them are excessive, he may make regulations setting the levels of charges.

Those levels must be no higher than those notified under sub-paragraph (2).

(6) If the Secretary of State makes regulations under sub-paragraph (5) no further submission to the Mayor of London under paragraph 3(1) may be made until after the end of the period of twelve months beginning with the day on which the regulations are made.

Publication of levels of charges

5 (1) Transport for London and the London local authorities shall publish, in such manner as the Mayor of London may determine, the levels of charges set in accordance with this Part of this Schedule.

(2) The duty imposed by sub-paragraph (1) applies—

(a) to Transport for London so far as the charges relate to contraventions on or adjacent to GLA roads, and

(b) to the London local authorities so far as they relate to—

(i) parking places provided or authorised by such authorities, or

(ii) contraventions on or adjacent to roads other than GLA roads.

Discharge of functions by London local authorities

6 (1) The Secretary of State may make provision by regulations as to the discharge by London local authorities of the functions conferred on them by this Part of this Schedule.

(2) The regulations may provide for the functions to be discharged by means of arrangements under section 101 of the Local Government Act 1972 (c. 70) (arrangements for discharge of functions by local authorities) or in such other way as the regulations may provide.

(3) The regulations may make provision for continuing in force for the purposes of this Part of this Schedule any arrangements in force immediately before the commencement of this Part for the discharge of functions corresponding to the functions of London local authorities under this Part of this Schedule.

PART 3

CHARGES APPLICABLE OUTSIDE GREATER LONDON

Charges to be set by enforcement authority

7 (1) Outside Greater London it is the duty of each enforcement authority to set the level of charges applicable in the case of contraventions for which they are the enforcement authority.

(2) Different levels of charges may be set for different parts of a civil enforcement area and for different cases or classes of case.

Guidelines given by appropriate national authority

8 (1) The levels of charges set by enforcement authorities under this Part of this Schedule must (subject to sub-paragraph (3)) accord with guidelines appended to an order made by the appropriate national authority.

(2) Different guidelines may be given for different cases or classes of case.

(3) An enforcement authority may, with the permission of the appropriate national authority, depart from any such guidelines.

Publication of levels of charges

9 An enforcement authority for an area outside Greater London shall publish, in such manner as the appropriate national authority may determine, the levels of charges set under this Part of this Schedule.

SCHEDULE 10

Section 84

CIVIL ENFORCEMENT: SPECIAL ENFORCEMENT AREAS

Designation of special enforcement areas in Greater London

1 (1) The Secretary of State may, on an application by a London authority, make an order designating the whole or part of that authority's area as a special enforcement area.

(2) An area may only be so designated if it is within, or is co-extensive with, an area that is a civil enforcement area for parking contraventions within paragraph 3 of Schedule 7 (parking contraventions other than those relating to parking places).

(3) An application under this paragraph may be made—

(a) by Transport for London, to the extent that the special enforcement area is to consist of GLA roads;

(b) by a London local authority, to the extent that the special enforcement area is to consist of roads other than GLA roads.

(4) Before making an order under this paragraph the Secretary of State shall consult the Commissioner of Police of the Metropolis or the Commissioner of Police for the City of London or, if appropriate, both of them.

(5) An order in force immediately before the commencement of this Part of this Act under section 76 of the Road Traffic Act 1991 (c. 40) designating an area in Greater London as a special parking area has effect on and after the commencement of this Part of this Act as if it were an order under this paragraph designating the area as a special enforcement area.

Variation of special enforcement area by Mayor of London

2 (1) The Mayor of London may by order under this paragraph amend an order for the time being in force under paragraph 1 so as to vary the area that for the time being constitutes the special enforcement area.

(2) No such order may be made without the consent of the relevant London authority for every road that the order has the effect of bringing within, or removing from, the special enforcement area.

(3) The relevant London authority is—

(a) as regards GLA roads, Transport for London;

(b) as regards roads other than GLA roads, the London local authority in whose area the road is situated.

(4) An order under this paragraph must not be such as to bring within a special enforcement area an area as to which the Secretary of State has specified by order that it is expedient on grounds of national security that no part of it should be included in a special enforcement area.

(5) An order in force immediately before the commencement of this Part of this Act under section 76A(1) or (3)(a) of the Road Traffic Act 1991 (c. 40) has effect on and after the commencement of this Part of this Act as if it made corresponding provision under this paragraph.

Designation of special enforcement areas outside Greater London

3 (1) The appropriate national authority may, on an application under this paragraph, make an order designating the whole or part of a local authority's area as a special enforcement area.

(2) An area may only be so designated if it is within, or is co-extensive with, an area that is a civil enforcement area for parking contraventions.

(3) An application under this paragraph may be made—

(a) with respect to the whole or part of their area, by a county council in England;

(b) with respect to the whole or part of their area, by a county council or county borough council in Wales;

(c) with respect to the whole of their area, by a metropolitan district council;

(d) with respect to the whole of their areas, by two or more metropolitan district councils acting jointly;

(e) with respect to the whole or part of the Isles of Scilly, by the Council of the Isles of Scilly.

(4) Before making an order under this paragraph the appropriate national authority shall consult the appropriate chief officer of police.

(5) An order in force immediately before the commencement of this Part of this Act under paragraph 2(1) of Schedule 3 to the Road Traffic Act 1991 designating an area outside Greater London as a special parking area has effect on and after the commencement of this Part of this Act as if it were an order under this paragraph designating the area as a special enforcement area.

SCHEDULE 11

Section 91

CIVIL ENFORCEMENT: CONSEQUENTIAL AMENDMENTS

Road Traffic Regulation Act 1984

1 (1) Section 46 of the Road Traffic Regulation Act 1984 (c. 27) (charges at, and regulation of, designated parking places) is amended as follows.

(2) In subsection (1) after "outside Greater London" insert ", and not in a civil enforcement area for parking contraventions,".

(3) In subsection (1A) after "in Greater London" insert ", or outside Greater London in a civil enforcement area for parking contraventions,".

(4) After subsection (5) add—

"(6) In this section "civil enforcement area for parking contraventions" has the same meaning as in Part 6 of the Traffic Management Act 2004.".

2 In section 63A of the Road Traffic Regulation Act 1984 (parking attendants), for subsection (4) (requirement to wear uniform) substitute—

"(4) Parking attendants in an area that is a civil enforcement area for parking contraventions—

(a) when exercising prescribed functions must wear such uniform as may be determined by the enforcement authority in accordance with guidance issued by the appropriate national authority, and

(b) must not exercise any of those functions when not in uniform.

Expressions used in this subsection that are defined for the purposes of Part 6 of the Traffic Management Act 2004 have the same meaning as in that Part.".

3 (1) In section 101 of the Road Traffic Regulation Act 1984 (disposal of vehicles removed under that Act)—

(a) in subsection (1) (power of competent authority to dispose of vehicle) for "Subject to subsections (3) to (5A) below" substitute "Subject to subsection (3) and section 101A below";

(b) omit subsections (4) to (6) (right of owner to recover vehicle or proceeds of sale).

(2) After that section insert—

"101A Right of owner to recover vehicle or proceeds of sale

"101A Right of owner to recover vehicle or proceeds of sale

(1) If before a vehicle is disposed of by an authority under section 101 above it is claimed by a person who—

(a) satisfies the authority that he is its owner, and

(b) pays the relevant charges,

the authority shall permit him to remove the vehicle from their custody within such period as they may specify or, in the case of an authority other than a local authority, as may be prescribed.

(2) If before the end of the period of one year beginning with the date on which a vehicle is sold by an authority under section 101 above a person satisfies the authority that at the time of the sale he was the owner of the vehicle, the authority shall pay him any sum by which the proceeds of sale exceed the amount of the relevant charges.

(3) In the case of a vehicle found in an area that is a civil enforcement area for parking contraventions, the relevant charges are—

(a) any penalty charge payable in respect of the parking of the vehicle in the place from which it was removed,

(b) such unpaid earlier penalty charges relating to the vehicle as may be prescribed, and

(c) such sums in respect of the removal and storage of the vehicle—

(i) as the authority may require in accordance with Schedule 9 of the Traffic Management Act 2004, or

(ii) in the case of an authority other than a local authority, as may be prescribed.

(4) In any other case the relevant charges are such sums in respect of the removal and storage of the vehicle as may be prescribed.

(5) If in the case of any vehicle it appears to the authority in question that more than one person is or was its owner at the relevant time, such one of them as the authority think fit shall be treated as its owner for the purposes of this section.

(6) In this section—

"civil enforcement area for parking contraventions" and "penalty charge" have the same meaning as in Part 6 of the Traffic Management Act 2004; and

"owner" has the same meaning as in section 101 above.

101B Representations and appeals

101B Representations and appeals

(1) The Lord Chancellor may make regulations entitling a person who in the case of a vehicle found in an area that is a civil enforcement area for parking contraventions—

(a) is required to pay an amount on recovering the vehicle under section 101A(1), or

(b) receives a sum in respect of the vehicle under section 101A(2) or is informed that the proceeds of sale did not exceed the aggregate amount mentioned in that provision,

to make representations to the authority concerned and to appeal to an adjudicator if his representations are not accepted.

(2) The regulations may make such provision in connection with the rights conferred as appears to the Lord Chancellor to be appropriate, and may in particular make provision—

(a) requiring the authority to give a person notice of the rights conferred by the regulations,

(b) as to the grounds on which, and time within which, representations may be made;

(c) requiring supporting evidence in such circumstances as may be specified;

(d) as to the duties of the authority when representations are received;

(e) as to the circumstances in which there is a right of appeal to an adjudicator,

(f) generally as to the making, determination and effect of, and procedure in connection with, such appeals, and

(g) enabling an adjudicator to review any decision made on, or in the course of, an appeal.

(3) The regulations may include provision authorising an adjudicator to require a person—

(a) to attend to give evidence at the hearing of an appeal, and

(b) to produce any documents in his custody or under his control relating to any matter relevant for the purposes of the appeal,

and making it a criminal offence triable summarily and punishable with a fine not exceeding level 2 on the standard scale to fail to comply with such a requirement.

(4) The regulations may include provision authorising an adjudicator to make an order for the payment of costs and expenses by a party to an appeal in such circumstances as may be specified.

(5) The functions of adjudicators under this section shall be discharged by the persons appointed as adjudicators for the purposes of Part 6 of the Traffic Management Act 2004 (civil enforcement of road traffic contraventions) and any arrangements made for the discharge of their functions under that Part also have effect for the purposes of this section.".

4 (1) Section 102 of the Road Traffic Regulation Act 1984 (c. 27) (charges for removal, storage and disposal of vehicles) is amended as follows.

(2) For subsection (2) (recovery of charges) substitute—

"(2) If the place from which the vehicle is removed is in an area that is not a civil enforcement area for parking contraventions—

(a) the appropriate authority is entitled to recover from any person responsible such charges as may be prescribed in respect of the removal of the vehicle;

(b) the chief officer of a police force or a local authority in whose custody the vehicle is during any period is entitled to recover from any person responsible charges ascertained by reference to a prescribed scale in respect of that period; and

(c) the chief officer of a police force or a local authority who dispose of the vehicle in pursuance of section 101 of this Act is entitled to recover from any person responsible charges determined in the prescribed manner in respect of its disposal.

(2A) If the place from which the vehicle is removed is in an area that is a civil enforcement area for parking contraventions, the enforcement authority is entitled to recover from any person responsible such charges in respect of the removal, storage and disposal of the vehicle as they may require in accordance with Schedule 9 of the Traffic Management Act 2004.".

(3) In subsection (8) (interpretation) at the appropriate place insert—

""civil enforcement area for parking contraventions" and "enforcement authority" have the same meaning as in Part 6 of the Traffic Management Act 2004;";

(4) In subsection (9) (application of provisions to parking places provided under letting or other arrangements), for "subsection (2)(d)" substitute "subsection (2A)".

Tribunals and Inquiries Act 1992

5 In Part 1 of Schedule 1 to the Tribunals and Inquiries Act 1992 (c. 53) (tribunals under direct supervision of Council on Tribunals), in paragraph 40 (road traffic) for sub-paragraph (b) substitute—

"(b) an adjudicator appointed for the purposes of Part 6 of the Traffic Management Act 2004 (civil enforcement of road traffic contraventions).".

London Local Authorities Act 1995

6 In the London Local Authorities Act 1995 (c. x)—

(a) in section 2 (interpretation), for the definition of "special parking area" substitute—

""special enforcement area" means a special enforcement area designated by order of the Secretary of State under Schedule 10 of the Traffic Management Act 2004;";

(b) in section 9(1) (special temporary prohibitions) for "special parking area" substitute "special enforcement area".

London Local Authorities and Transport for London Act 2003

7 In section 20 of the London Local Authorities and Transport for London Act 2003 (c. iii) (disclosure of information about identity of owner of vehicle), in subsection (2) (enactments for purposes of which disclosure may be made) for paragraphs (b) to (d) substitute—

"(b) Part 6 of the Traffic Management Act 2004 (civil enforcement of road traffic contraventions).".

SCHEDULE 12

Section 98

REPEALS

PART 1

CIVIL ENFORCEMENT

Short title and chapter	*Extent of repeal*
Road Traffic Regulation Act 1984 (c. 27)	Section 8(1A) and (1B).
	Section 11(2) and (2A).
	In section 47(1), the words "; but this subsection does not apply in relation to any designated parking place in Greater London".
	Section 101(4) to (6).
	In section 102(8), the definition of "London authority" and the word "and" preceding it.
Road Traffic Act 1988 (c. 52)	Section 36(1A).
Road Traffic Act 1991 (c. 40)	Section 43.
	Sections 65 to 67.
	Section 68(2) and (3)(c).
	Sections 69 to 74A.
	Sections 76 to 79.
	Schedule 3.
	Schedule 6.
Local Government Wales Act 1994 (c. 19)	In Schedule 7, paragraph 43(b).
London Local Authorities Act 1995 (c. x)	Sections 4, 5, 7 and 8.
Greater London Authority Act 1999 (c. 29)	Section 283(2) and (4).
	Section 284.
	Section 286.
Transport Act 2000 (c. 38)	Section 144.
London Local Authorities Act 2000 (c. vii)	In section 3(1), the definition of "special parking area".
	Sections 4 to 14.
London Local Authorities and Transport for London Act 2003 (c. iii)	Sections 4 to 7.
	Sections 14 and 15.
	Schedule 1.
	In Schedule 2—

Short title and chapter	*Extent of repeal*
	(a) in the heading, the words from "4" to "and"; (b) paragraph 1(a); (c) paragraphs 5 and 6.
	Schedule 3.

PART 2

OTHER REPEALS

Short title and chapter	*Extent of repeal*
Road Traffic Offenders Act 1988 (c. 53)	In Schedule 1, in column 2 of the entry relating to section 163 of the Road Traffic Act 1988 the words "by constable".
	In Part 1 of Schedule 2, in column 2 of the entry relating to section 37 of the Road Traffic Act 1988 the words "by constable regulating traffic", and in column 2 of the entry relating to section 163 of the Road Traffic Act 1988 the words "by constable".
	In Schedule 3, in column 2 of the entry relating to section 163 of the Road Traffic Act 1988 the words "by constable in uniform".
London Local Authorities and Transport for London Act 2003 (c. iii)	Section 12.

Adapted and published by GRANGIS under the OGL Licence 3.0.

www.nationalarchives.gov.uk/doc/open-government-licence/version/3/

GRANGIS - UK PUBLISHING 2022.

Thank you for taking the time to leave us a review regarding this version

★★★★★

For further inquiries, contact us at:
www.grangis.com / contact@grangis.com

www.ingramcontent.com/pod-product-compliance
Lightning Source LLC
LaVergne TN
LVHW060213210926
848481LV00008B/2724